Essex, Suffolk and Norfolk

LEN BANISTER, GEOFF PRATT
AND WILL MARTIN

COUNTRYSIDE BOOKS
NEWBURY BERKSHIRE

First published 2005

© Len Banister, Geoff Pratt & Will Martin, 2005

COUNTRYSIDE BOOKS
3 Catherine Road
Newbury, Berkshire

To view our complete range of books,
please visit us at
www.countrysidebooks.co.uk

ISBN 1 85306 899 3

Photographs by the authors

Image of Rattlesden on the front cover
supplied by Mark Mitchels

Designed by Peter Davies, Nautilus Design
Produced through MRM Associates Ltd., Reading
Typeset by Techniset Typesetters, Newton-le-Willows
Printed by Woolnough Bookbinding Ltd., Irthlingborough

Contents

INTRODUCTION
WALKS IN ESSEX

1. **Arkesden:** The Axe and Compasses (2½ or 5½ miles)   7
2. **Birchanger:** The Three Willows (4 miles)   10
3. **Stapleford Tawney:** The Mole Trap (5¼ miles)   13
4. **Ashdon:** The Rose and Crown (5¼ miles)   16
5. **Mill Green:** The Viper (3 miles)   19
6. **Horndon on the Hill:** The Bell (6¾, 5¾ or 3½ miles)   22
7. **Stock:** The Hoop (3¾ miles)   26
8. **Fuller Street:** The Square and Compasses (5¼ miles)   29
9. **Great Yeldham:** The White Hart (3½ miles)   32
10. **Castle Hedingham:** The Bell (5½ miles)   35
11. **Gosfield:** The Green Man (5 miles)   38
12. **Stow Maries:** The Prince of Wales (7 miles)   41
13. **Paglesham Eastend:** The Plough & Sail (5½ miles)   44
14. **Fingringhoe:** The Whalebone (4½ miles)   47

WALKS IN SUFFOLK

15. **Icklingham:** The Red Lion (6 or 6¾ miles)   50
16. **Long Melford:** The Black Lion (5 miles)   53
17. **Bures:** The Swan Inn (5½ miles)   57
18. **Felsham:** The Six Bells (4½ miles)   60
19. **Polstead:** The Cock (4 miles)   63
20. **Rickinghall:** The White Horse (6 or 5 miles)   66
21. **East Bergholt:** The Red Lion (5 miles)   69
22. **Thorndon:** The Black Horse Inn (6½ miles)   72
23. **Little Bealings:** The Admiral's Head (5 miles)   75
24. **Fressingfield:** The Swan (5½ miles)   78
25. **Framlingham:** The Castle Inn (3 miles)   81
26. **Bungay:** The Fleece (5½ miles)   84
27. **Butley:** The Oyster Inn (5½ or 6¼ miles)   87
28. **Thorpeness:** The Dolphin (4½ miles)   90

Contents

WALKS IN NORFOLK

29. **Stowbridge:** The Heron (5½ miles)   93

30. **Bawsey:** The Sandboy (4 miles)   96

31. **Hockwold cum Wilton:** The Red Lion (6½ miles)   99

32. **Helhoughton:** The Sculthorpe Mill (3 miles)   102

33. **Cley next the Sea:** The Three Swallows (4 or 5¾ miles)   105

34. **Old Buckenham:** The Gamekeeper (5 miles)   108

35. **Colton:** The Ugly Bug Inn (3 miles)   111

36. **Scole:** The Scole Inn (4 miles)   114

37. **Aldborough:** The Old Red Lion (4 miles)   117

38. **Crostwick:** The White Horse (5 miles)   120

39. **Martham:** The Fisherman's Return, Winterton-on-Sea (4½ miles)   123

40. **Chedgrave:** The White Horse (4½ miles)   126

PUBLISHER'S NOTE

We hope that you obtain considerable enjoyment from this book; great care has been taken in its preparation. Although at the time of publication all routes followed public rights of way or permitted paths, diversion orders can be made and permissions withdrawn.

We cannot, of course, be held responsible for such diversion orders and any inaccuracies in the text which result from these or any other changes to the routes nor any damage which might result from walkers trespassing on private property. We are anxious though that all details covering the walks are kept up to date and would therefore welcome information from readers which would be relevant to future editions.

The simple sketch maps that accompany the walks in this book are based on notes made by the author whilst checking the routes on the ground. They are designed to show you how to reach the start and to point out the main features of the overall circuit, and they contain a progression of numbers that relate to the paragraphs of the text.

However, for the benefit of a proper map, we do recommend that you purchase the relevant Ordnance Survey sheet covering your walk. The Ordnance Survey maps are widely available, especially through booksellers and local newsagents.

Area map showing locations of the walks

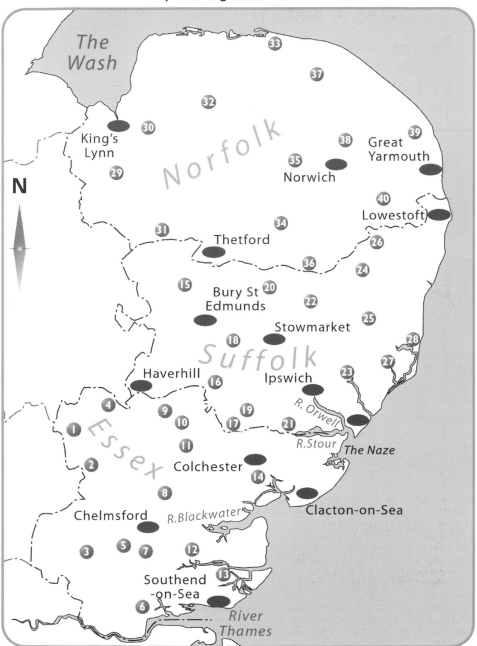

Introduction

Everybody walks for pleasure at some time or another. That pleasure is immeasurably heightened when you gain the confidence to walk deep into the countryside using the myriad of public footpaths which criss-cross the fields and woods linking farms and churches with the hamlets and villages that surround our town and cities. The counties of Essex, Suffolk and Norfolk offer a rich store of wonderful walks along such paths.

Essex has the most extensive network of footpaths and the longest coastline of any county. Its ancient royal hunting forests, its beautiful villages and numerous castles more than make up for its lack of mountains and moorland. Whilst Suffolk, with its large tracts of forest, heathland and lush pastures has a huge variety of landscapes to delight the eye. Norfolk has its fair share of coastline but it is its range of riverside paths that prove its biggest attraction. Its saltmarshes and reed-fringed broads are a bird spotter's paradise.

The selection of walks described here offer a good introduction to each of these counties for visitors and residents alike. Each walk starts from a good pub and follows a route carefully selected for its intrinsic interest. The pubs range from the simple, old-fashioned country pub to the large successful dining establishment but what is common to all is that they serve well-kept beers and excellent food. Using country pubs also helps to preserve this uniquely British institution; so you will be enjoying yourself and putting something back into the countryside. Just as wine complements food, we hope that the pubs will complement the walks.

Most of the pubs are happy for you to leave your cars in their car parks whilst walking but do seek permission first and of course, this is usually on the understanding that you will be calling in for a drink or a meal on your return. If you do park on the road, please do so with consideration for local residents.

Each of the 40 circular walks is accompanied by a sketch map giving an overview of the route to be followed though for greater detail it is recommended that you also arm yourself with the relevant OS map for the area.

Finally, we hope you derive as much pleasure from these routes as we have had in devising them.

Len Banister, Geoff Pratt
and Will Martin

The Axe and Compasses

post office all sitting on a main street bordered by a seasonal stream, so that the houses on one side have to be approached by a series of bridges. The walk follows some of the best field-edge paths in the county to a second village, Clavering. Here the houses are grander but no less attractive, and we pass by an ancient castle site and a beautiful church. For those who wish it, a much shorter option is available.

Arkesden is one of those villages which seem to have been produced by a public relations department acting on behalf of rural Britain. It has thatched cottages, a church, pub and a

The Axe and Compasses dates from 1650, although it has since been enlarged to accommodate a restaurant and a superb public bar, which was added in the early 1900s. The lounge bar is the epitome of comfort. The extensive and reasonably priced menu contains a mixture of adventurous and standard bar food. You can expect to see meals like bangers and mash alongside grilled salmon fillet with asparagus, butter, cream and white wine. Vegetarians are well catered for with a whole range of dishes such as spinach and potato cakes. Real ales include Greene King IPA, Abbot and Speckled Hen.

Distance: 5½ or 2½ miles

OS Explorer 194: Hertford and Bishop's Stortford.
GR 484344

There are some gentle undulations but nothing severe. The paths are excellent, making this a walk for all seasons.

Starting point: The pub car park. Please ask the landlord for permission before leaving your car whilst you walk.

How to get there: If you are coming from the east, turn off the B1383 (which runs parallel to the M11) on either the B1039 or B1038, and follow signs at the first junctions. From the west these two roads can be accessed from the A10.

Opening times from Monday to Saturday are 11.30 am (noon on Saturday) to 2.30 pm and from 6 pm to 11 pm; on Sunday from noon to 3 pm and from 7 pm to 11 pm. Bar food is available from noon to 2 pm and from 6.45 pm to 9.30 pm (none on Sunday evenings in winter).

Telephone: 01799 550272.

The Walk

1 Go left along the road from the pub. Passing a junction which would take you to the church, continue to the outskirts of the village and beyond. Just before the national speed limit sign, turn left to walk up a field with a hedge on your left. (You pass a series of five groves of trees on your left – the most improbably named is Knock 'emdown Grove.) After about ½ mile, keep with the field edge as it makes

some elaborate swings from right to left before reaching a junction.

2 Go left, keeping subsequent groves on the left. Diagonally right is a sail-less windmill and ahead is a fishing lake. When you have walked ⅓ of a mile you will come to a wide cross-track.

3 Turn right (*unless you are doing the short walk, in which case follow the directions from point 8*). Walk with a

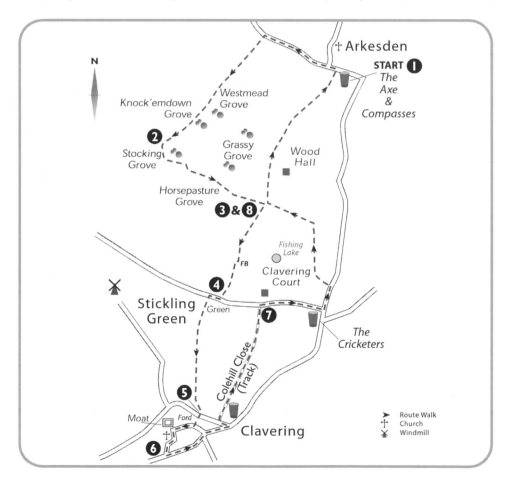

hedge on your left. Where the track curves right, carry straight on but now on the left side of the hedge. After 40 yards, go right over a plank bridge and continue along on the field edge, which goes left and eventually takes you on a short, hedged path which leads onto a road at Stickling Green.

❹ Turn right and walk a short distance along the road before turning left at a concrete fingerpost. Follow the direction indicated and you will go along a narrow path between houses and emerge, via a bridge, in a field. Go ahead on a path which follows a line of telegraph poles across a field. Continue ahead across the next field to reach the first stile of the day. This takes you onto a path by a wooden fence to arrive at another stile and then a lane.

❺ Go ahead over a bridge alongside a ford and walk up a street between sympathetically renovated Tudor houses. At the top, turn right along The Bury, passing manicured holly hedges and pleasant homes along the way. Go through the gate to the churchyard. Go left, passing the 14th century church on your right (well worth a visit). Leave the churchyard via an elaborate wood and metal gate and walk between leaning houses.

❻ At the road, turn left and continue along the main road to pass the village

Returning to Arkesden

sign on your left. At the 40 mph sign, turn left and then right up a path alongside Colehill Close; it develops into a path which takes you across a field to a road.

❼ Turn right, passing Clavering Court on the left, to reach a road junction. Turn left along the road, and, just after Summer House, go left along a narrow path; walk down past its boundary and enter a field. Go diagonally right to a gap and then right along the field-edge. At the end of the field follow the edge left to reach a cross-track, which you should recognize.

❽ Go right here (left, if you are on the short walk). When the track forks, leave it and carry on ahead along a field edge with a hedge on your right. The path returns you to Arkesden, where you turn right to return to the pub.

Date walk completed:

....

Place of Interest
In nearby Newport, at the western end of the main road near the station, is **R. & R. Sagger**, a rather superior garden centre which specializes in unusual plants and statuary. Whatever your interest in gardening you are bound to find something to fascinate you while walking around the comparatively small area. It is open every day except Monday, 10 am to 5 pm.

9

The Three Willows

This short walk starts in Birchanger and takes you through historic Stansted Mountfitchet, yet still manages to include some woodland and pasture. You have ample time to pick out the various attractions of this large village as you approach from the south. Once in the streets, anyone with a passing interest in domestic architecture will, on the one hand, wonder at some beautifully preserved examples and, on the other, be amazed at the horrors perpetrated in the name of modernization. The reconstructed Norman village in the centre is a great tourist draw, and the windmill which is passed on the return is an important local landmark.

Like other out-of-the-way pubs featured in this book, the popularity of the **Three Willows** demonstrates the way in which discerning customers are prepared to travel for quality. The 'willows' of the name refers to the three styles of cricket bat which are featured on the inn sign. This is a roomy, comfortable place which serves real ales to accompany simple, well cooked and very reasonably priced bar meals. Besides the usual pub fare, you can expect items such as fish crumble and bacon and onion pudding to be on the menu. It's best to book if you want to eat in the restaurant.

Opening times on Monday to Saturday are from 11.30 am to 3 pm and from 6 pm to 11 pm, and on Sunday from noon to 3 pm and 7 pm to 11 pm.

Telephone: 01279 815913.

Distance: *4 miles*

OS Explorer 195 Braintree and Saffron Walden
GR 513224

Nearly half this walk is along surfaced lanes and roads; even so, parts of the outward route can become muddy after rain.

Starting point: The pub car park. In spite of notices warning you of wheel-clamping, the landlord is quite happy for you to park at the pub whilst you walk as long as you return with your custom.

How to get there: Leave the M11 at junction 8 (for Bishop's Stortford) on the A120, and then turn right at the first roundabout. The Three Willows is about ½ mile along the road.

The Walk

❶ Move off to the right from the Three Willows car park and, after a few yards, turn right into a lane and almost immediately left to walk alongside a field. At the end of the field, continue ahead to the right of a recreation ground and up a narrow fenced path to reach a building. Go left and right around the building and go right onto a lane. The lane dwindles into a stony footpath. Where this forks, go just inside the edge of the wood but maintain your direction. At the end of the wood go left and then

right to join a path along a field edge and keep ahead towards a prominent barn in front of Parsonage Farm. You will reach a lane in front of the barn.

❷ Turn left to walk for about ¼ mile along Parsonage Lane, from which you can view Stansted Mountfitchet. You then come to a road.

❸ Cross the road and walk up a narrow path into woodland. Keep to the main path. As you emerge from trees, ignore the first left fork but take the second, and, after 3 yards, go right and walk to the

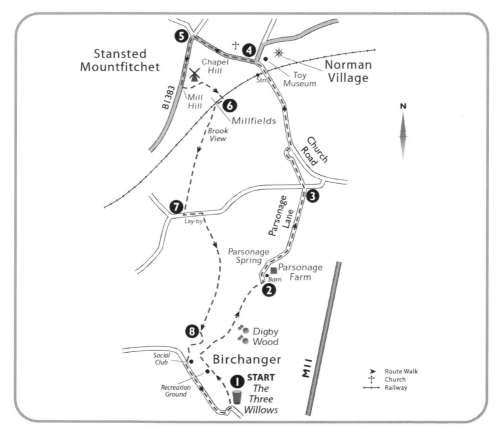

11

right of a Scots pine, into scrub. Keep going right, beside the boundary of a house, to cross a stream and climb up to a road. Cross over and turn left to walk into Stansted along the pavement of Church Road, passing some stylish houses along the way. (Stop on the middle of the railway bridge to see the Norman village on the raised ground over to the right.) You reach a major crossroads. (If you want to visit the Norman village you should go right here, up Lower Street.)

❹ Cross over and walk up Chapel Hill. (Notice the grand United Reformed Church.) At the top of the hill you reach the main road.

❺ Turn left and continue to a turning signed 'Mill Hill to Millside'. Go left here to walk up to the windmill. (Open on the afternoon of the first Sunday of the month from April to October.) Continue along Millside and then go right, down Millfields. At the bottom, go ahead to the left of a gate to go by a narrow path over a footbridge. Turn left at the T-junction and take the next turning on the right, which will take you to a bridge over the railway.

❻ Once across, go right, through a small estate. At the end, go diagonally right along the right-hand side of Brook View. Then go to the right of a barrier joining a narrow tree-lined path. The path later continues alongside a track, and, after about ¹/₃ mile, you reach a road.

❼ Turn left. At a lay-by on the right, look for a fingerpost leading you through a gate. Walk up the left-hand side of the field. At the top left corner, go through another gate and walk up the left edge of

The United Reformed Church, Stansted Mountfichet

the next field. Continue, with a wood on your left. Keep ahead at a junction of tracks and walk towards a line of houses. When you reach these, go left and immediately right.

❽ Go right and round to the left to arrive at a T-junction, where you turn right. Go left at the next T-junction, passing Birchanger Social Club on your left, to reach the main road. Go left and follow the road for ¼ mile to return to the pub.

Places of Interest

Stansted Mountfitchet castle. Attractions include reconstructions of a smithy, an alchemist and candlemaker's, a brewhouse, a pottery, a weaving and dyeing house, a chicken house, a dovecote and a falconry.

Next door is the **House on the Hill Toy Museum**, a vast collection of over 30,000 toys, games, and children's books from the late Victorian period to the 1970s. There is a shop where toys can be bought and sold. Telephone: 01279 813237.

Date walk completed:

....

Stapleford Tawney 3 `Walk`

The Mole Trap

amazed that you can so quickly evade most other signs of modern civilization as you pass along quiet lanes into ancient woodland to join a section of the Essex Way, a trail which leads right across Essex from Harwich to Epping. Later you will be able to see the icons of the commercial centre of London in the distance, far removed from your own bucolic surroundings of meadows and woods.

This walk provides an extraordinary and immediate escape into the countryside. Although you will encounter the M11 twice, you will be

Distance: 5¼ miles

OS Explorer 183 (just the edge) and 174
GR 501013

An undulating walk but nothing too steep; some paths can become quite muddy in periods of heavy or prolonged rainfall

Starting point: The car park of the Mole Trap. The landlord is quite happy for you to park here as long as you use the pub.

How to get there: Turn off the A113 to Stapleford Tawney at Passingford Bridge (just north of the M25 overpass). Tawney Common is a mile or so past Stapleford Tawney; just keep going and you will reach the pub.

Although it seems to be in the back of beyond, the **Mole Trap** is always busy. It has a low ceiling and is comfortably furnished. The staple beer is Fuller's London Pride but there is always an interesting selection of at least three guest ales. The food is well prepared and unpretentious, with dishes such as chilli con carne, lasagne, and steak. There is always fresh fish on the menu, and sandwiches and a roast are available on Sundays; no food is served on Sunday evenings, however.

Opening times from Monday to Saturday are 11.30 am to 3 pm and 6.30 pm to 11 pm; and from noon to 4 pm and 6.30 pm to 10.30 pm on Sunday.

Telephone: 01992 522394.

13

The Walk

① With your back to the pub turn right to walk down the quiet country lane for just over ¼ mile. On reaching a T-junction, turn left and then soon turn right to go to the back of a small car park and onward through woodland to emerge on a field edge with the wood on your left. Soon you reach a cross track in front of a clump of trees on the brow of this gentle hill.

② Turn left to start on a ¾ mile section of delightful, but often muddy, mixed woodland. At a cross track you will notice banks which are believed to be field

boundaries dating back to the 11th century (they also do a good job in thwarting the progress of 4x4 vehicles); here you continue ahead on the footpath signed to Gernon Bushes. Notice that the woodland has now taken on a different character, the predominant species now being birch – hence the name Birching Coppice. Cross a bridge over the mill.

③ A few yards down from the bridge go left at a wooden barrier so that you are now walking parallel with the motorway. At a waymarker swing right downhill through an area of trees which were pollarded long ago, to reach the bottom of a valley. Fork left; then go right over a

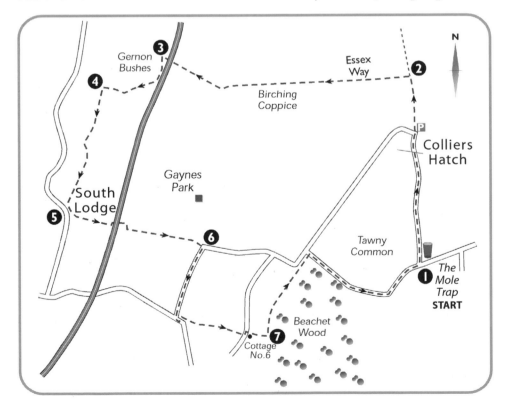

tiny bridge and walk uphill. The path drifts nearer and nearer to the left edge of the wood as it climbs. At a junction with a waymarker post turn left to cross a sleeper bridge and a stile.

4 Go forward along the right-hand edge of a field. Ahead there are extensive views of Loughton and Abridge. Halfway along the next field, at a marker post, fork diagonally left and walk to a gap in the hedge ahead. Once through, keep to the right hand edge of the field. Go through another gap to go straight ahead into trees to reach a road.

5 Turn left and continue through a gate to the right of the drive passing South Lodge. At the end of this narrow field you cross a bridge and walk up the left edge of a much larger field. In the top left-hand corner you will find a gate which will take you to the bridge by which you re-cross the motorway. Once across, if you look up to the left you should catch a glimpse of Gaynes Park. Turn right for about 15 yards and then go left and along the edge of another extensive field. Go down to a dip, through a hedge, and continue climbing. You emerge on a road.

6 Turn right. Although this is a moderately busy stretch of road, for most of the way you can walk along a wide grass verge. At the T-junction, turn left in the direction of Theydon Mount and after about 15 yards veer left on a short track to go right along a field edge. When the hedge on the right ends, continue onward across the remainder of the field and through a gap in the hedge. Continue with a shallow ditch on the right to reach a pathway with a stile and pass between traditional and modern buildings

In June the rhododendrons which line the path are in flower

to arrive at a lane. Turn left and then right and walk alongside cottage number 6, through a fence and up to woodland along the right-hand edge of a field.

7 On reaching the woodland, turn left and walk with the wood on your right and extensive views opening up on the left. Continue on this undulating path past several boundaries, to reach a road and turn right. Follow the road for about ½ mile as it swings left and returns you to the Mole Trap.

Place of Interest
Blake Hall Gardens are north-west of Chipping Ongar, off the A414, which you can reach by returning to the A113 and turning left. A garden walk takes in a tropical house, an ornamental wood, an ice house and a bog garden. Situated in the south wing of Blake Hall is a war museum. Various events and exhibitions are also held in the house and grounds. Telephone: 01277 364694.

Date walk completed:

....

15

The Rose and Crown

A beautiful village, a windmill, some wonderful country houses, the highest burial mounds in Britain – what more could you want from a walk? Well, this one also offers extensive views across the valley of the River Bourn and a return to a pub which is steeped in history.

The Rose and Crown was built in the early 17th century and has hardly changed over the last 400 years. The Cromwell room, to the right of the main bar, appears at first sight to be decoratively panelled, but closer inspection reveals that the panels are painted on the walls; they were the work of Royalist prisoners kept here by Cromwell during the Civil War and were only exposed during restoration work. The pub serves a good range of beers, which includes Ridleys IPA. There is the usual basic fare of sandwiches and jacket potatoes, but it is worth trying the more ambitious menu, which might include mushroom nut roast, served on a bed of sweet red pepper sauce, or chicken supreme with Parma ham and a tomato and pasta sauce. If you are feeling really hungry, go for the cod and chips, which is the largest you will get east of Slapton Sands.

Distance: *5¼ miles*

OS Explorer 209 Cambridge, Royston, Duxford and Linton
GR 586421

This is a gently undulating walk mainly over tracks and field edges.

Starting point: The car park of the Rose and Crown. The landlord is happy for you to leave your car whilst you walk, provided that you also give the pub your custom.

How to get there: Turn off the A1307 near Linton for Bartlow; Ashdon is signed. The pub is at the major crossroads in the village.

Opening times are from 12 noon to 2.30 pm Tuesday to Saturday (closed Monday lunchtime) and 6 pm to 11 pm Monday to Saturday. Sunday hours are noon to 4 pm and 7 pm to 10.30 pm.

Telephone: 01799 584337.

The Walk

1 Leave the pub car park and turn left along the road to walk through the village, passing the war memorial and allotments, and turn right at a concrete footpath sign just as the road swings to the left. Enter a field, turn left, and follow the field edge. At the top of this field, go through a narrow gap and continue up a second field.

2 Leave the field by the left-hand corner and turn right onto a lane. Soon you arrive at Bragg's Mill, built in 1757 and

currently being restored by a charitable trust formed by the villagers. On the left-hand side of the lane, opposite the mill, are two footpath signs. Take the left-hand path and go diagonally across the field to reach a hedge, where you turn left into woodland. At a T-junction at the end of the wood, turn left to go over a stile and keep forward with the wood on the left. Towards the end of the field, swing right and descend to a road.

3 Turn left. Just past a large barn, go right through white gates and along an impressive drive. (Soon you pass Waltons,

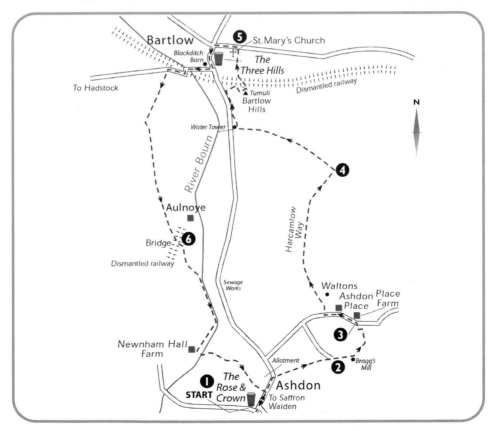

a more recent but very handsome building). Continue along the tree-lined drive. (You are now on the Harcamlow Way, a long-distance path between Harlow and Cambridge.) After about $\frac{1}{3}$ mile the drive splits; go straight ahead here between hedges and join a field-edge track. When the hedge on the right ends, continue along the broad grassy track, which, swinging gradually to the right, brings you alongside another section of woodland. Keep on to the top of the hill, with a hedge on the skyline.

❹ Turn left to walk down the valley side, with the hedge on your right. After about ½ mile you approach a road. About 20 yards before it, turn right to walk past a fine circular, brick-built water tower and swing left before a dovecote. Again you approach the road; this time, about 3 yards before it, turn right up some steps to join a meandering path through ivy-clad trees. Cross a deep cross-track and then turn right along a narrow fenced path. At the end, the first of the Bartlow Hills appears on your right. One of the first two hills is fenced, if you walk around this you will come to a flight of steps to its top. From the steps go left along the site boundary fence, past the third mound, and cross a brick bridge over a disused railway. Keep following the path between garden walls and fences, across a bridge, and into the churchyard of St Mary's, with its round tower.

❺ Leaving the churchyard, turn left into the road. At the first junction, go left on the Ashdon road, passing the Three Hills pub and Blackditch Barn before reaching a second junction, where you go right on the road signed to Hadstock. Soon after crossing the River Bourne, the road goes

between the remains of a railway bridge. Keep on the road until you reach woodland and a footpath sign on the left. Climb steadily up the track. About halfway between the wood you have passed and another ahead, go left to follow a cross field track. Ignore a path going to the right (opposite Aulnoye, an isolated building surrounded by hedges, on your left), and keep ahead towards the valley floor, the route having been joined by a drive from the house before crossing another railway bridge.

❻ Eventually the track becomes surfaced, and you can see a sewage farm ahead, don't cross the bridge before it but turn right through a gap in the hedge and walk along the field edge with the river on your left. Continue into a second field by a stile. Where the hedge swings to the left, keep straight on to another stile and turn right up a drive to Newnham Hall Farm. Go past houses; turn left in front of farm buildings; and go left again at an open barn and through a double gate. Stay on this track, with the hedge on your right, until, just before the end of the field, you go through a gate and down a drive to the main road. Turn right to return to the Rose and Crown.

Place of Interest
Ashdon Village Museum lies further down the road, south of the pub. It is a wonderfully eclectic exhibition of village life, based on the artefacts and photographs collected by a local boy. Telephone: 01799 584452.

Date walk completed:
....

Distance: *3 miles*

OS Explorer 183 Chelmsford and The Rodings
GR 641017

Given that there is a lot of walking across and along the edges of fields, this is not as muddy as might be expected. All gradients are very gentle.

Starting point: The Viper pub. There is public car parking on the edge of woodland on the opposite side of the road to the pub.

How to get there: Mill Green is not the easiest place to reach. A careful look at the road map before making your trip will repay the effort. If you are on the A414 between Writtle and Chipping Ongar, you need to turn off (south) to Loves Green and then follow signs to Fryering. From the A12 between Brentwood and Chelmsford, turn off on the B1002. In the middle of Ingatestone take a very narrow road, Fryering Lane, north-west between houses. Go right at major junctions; the Viper is north of the green in Mill Green.

The area surrounding Mill Green is probably the best in Essex for catching sight of deer. On this walk you will have a really good chance of seeing them in the open rather just glimpsing them in woodland. This short walk takes you around and through woodland, across open fields and provides good views over the surrounding countryside. It is the ideal route for a relaxing summer evening or a crisp morning in winter.

The Viper is the ideal stop for those who hanker for the country pub of times past. The rooms are beautifully simple with plain floors, panelled walls and built-in benches. The orange/yellow varnish finish looks better than it sounds. The private bar is also uncluttered, though it is carpeted and the seating is upholstered, providing a perfectly comfortable environment, with an open fire in winter. The food is limited in range, fairly basic, but of good value. You can get a local sausage with onions in a roll, and substantial pies. The pièce de résistance is the range of chilli dishes of various challenging strengths. A major attraction is the range of beers, which includes the products of Essex brewers Ridleys and Mighty Oak.

Opening times all week are from noon to 3 pm and from 6 pm to 11 pm (7 pm to 10.30 pm on Sunday evening).

Telephone: 01277 352010.

The Walk

1 With your back to the Viper, leave the car park by the surfaced lane, which swings right and left. Fork left along a gravelled drive past a house and continue to a barrier, where you go left to walk just inside the edge of a wood for a short distance. Climb a stile and continue alongside the wood, but now in a field. Two more stiles bring you to the far end of Box Wood and into another field.

2 Turn right along the hedge until this turns off. Keep across the field, going slightly left towards a stile. (Over on the right is a fishing lake; if the path is not obvious, walk to the hedge opposite and follow this round until you come to the stile on your right.) Once over the stile, follow the field edge along for about 50 yards; then, at the corner, fork right across the field, aiming for the right of Dawes Farm. Walk past the farm, ignoring the stile on the right. At the corner of a leylandii hedge, strike off diagonally left across the field to a stile and plank bridge. Then continue ahead to a gap in a hedge to reach a lane.

3 Turn right and follow the lane between Handley Green Farm buildings and past a couple of ponds. Just after a row of stables on the left, turn right along a track at a concrete footpath sign. Within a few yards the track forks, go left following a field boundary on your right. At the bottom of the field turn right and walk along a field with the hedge on your right. (You will notice from the signpost that you pass that you are now on St Peter's Way, a 43-mile walk from Chipping Ongar to Bradwell.) Just before Bushey Wood, turn left across a bridge and then right to re-cross the stream. Walk just inside the edge of the wood. (Here you will notice feeding hoppers, wire fences and shelters – all connected with the raising of game birds.) Leave the wood by a stile and keep along

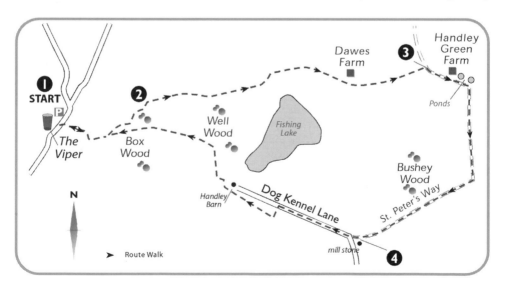

Deer seen on the walk

the left edge of a field. Cross a stile and continue to another stile at the end of the next field to reach a lane. (Notice the old mill stone on the left.)

4 Turn right along Dog Kennel Lane. At a hedge, turn left and cross a double stile and bridge a short way along on the right. Go right along the edge of a field, passing the attractive buildings of Handley Barns, and cross a stile to go downhill beside a ditch. Ignoring a bridge on the left, cross another stile into a field. Go right along the field edge and left with the edge of Well Wood. Where this ends, continue across the field to a stile which takes you into a second wood. Go along a path, guided occasionally by waymarkers.

Eventually swing right to a barrier, which you may recognize from your outward trip. Go through, following the gravel path, and turn right on the surfaced track to return to the car parking area.

Place of Interest
Ingatesone Hall, in nearby Ingatestone, is a 16th-century mansion built by Sir William Petre, who was a secretary of state to four monarchs. Telephone: 01277 353010.

Date walk completed:

....

21

Horndon on the Hill
The Bell

and climbing through woodland and pasture, you get the chance to enjoy extensive views over to Kent from the Westley Heights. I have included some alternatives for those who want a shorter outing.

The Bell is thought by many to be one of the best pubs in Britain. It is an old coaching inn, with a medieval hall which serves as a restaurant. You enter via a comfortable traditional bar with panelled walls, which has changed little in the last 60 years. Here you can choose from a good selection of real ales, including Bass served by gravity directly from the cask. The bar food area, which adjoins the restaurant, serves food on a first-come-first-served basis as opposed to the restaurant where booking is recommended. The food is not cheap, but it is wonderful. You might have smoked haddock risotto with boiled egg and parsley as a starter, followed by roast quail with black pudding and girolles, and finish with apricot tarte tartin with maple lavender ice cream. Unless you are eating in the restaurant you need to arrive early, especially at weekends.

Leaving this isolated village, which has a number of superb old buildings at its centre, the walk takes you out over the flats, which would have been the old flood plains of the Thames Estuary. Soon turning inland

Distance: *6¾ miles, 5¾ miles or 3½ miles.*

OS Explorer 175 Southend on Sea and Basildon.
GR 670832

The short walk is completely flat. The longer alternatives climb steadily to Westley Heights and have one short steep descent.

Starting point: The car park of the Bell Inn. The owners are happy for you to park there as long as you visit the pub before or after your walk.

How to get there: Horndon on the Hill is on a turning off the southern end of the B1007, which runs between the A127 and the A13.

Opening times from Monday to Saturday are 11 am to 2.30 pm (3 pm Saturday) and 5.30 pm (6 pm Saturday) to 11 pm; Sunday 12 noon to 4 pm and 7 pm to 10.30 pm. Bar food is available 12 noon to 2 pm and 6.30 pm to 9.45 pm.

Telephone: 01375 642463.

The Walk

1 Leave the Bell car park and turn right to walk down the High Road. After passing allotments, fork right to reach a road, which you cross. Walk left along the verge for about 40 yards, looking for a gap in the hedge on the right.

2 Cross a stile and go diagonally left across the field to a bridge in the hedge. Once across, go straight ahead to a stile on the other side of the field. In the next field go diagonally to the far right-hand corner and cross a stile and a couple of bridges. Then go diagonally left to the far corner. Now walk up the field edge, with the hedge on the left, cross a stile and continue onward, with a track to the left; then walk to the right of a hedge. At the end of this, go left over a stile and turn right along a wide grassy track; where this swings sharply to the left before a hedge, carry straight on, through the first gap,

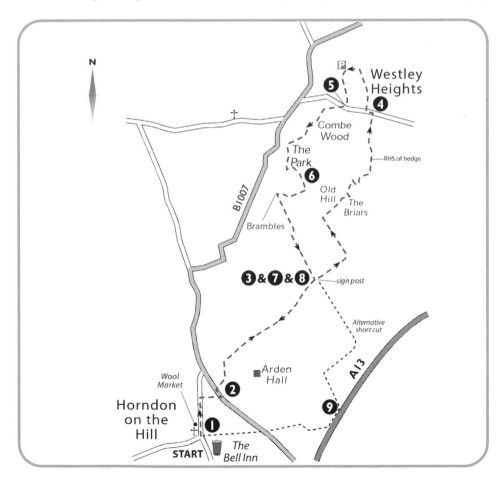

across an earthen bridge and up the left edge of the field. Climb a stile into woodland.

3 Almost immediately you encounter a signpost. *If you wish to take the short walk, go directly to point 8.* Otherwise, turn right, and, after about 10 yards, go left up the right inside of the wood before eventually swinging left out onto a field corner. Continue along footpath 86, which goes through the centre of the vast field to your left, aiming for a gap about 50 yards to the right of a bungalow. Once through the gap in the hedge, go right along a track. Just before gates to the Briars and Milo, go left into woodland and then right on a surfaced ride. When the ride starts to go downhill and you reach a junction, go left uphill and, after a few yards, turn right; go down through a gate, and, following the yellow arrows, trace the field edge round and up beside a farm. Pass through a metal kissing gate and go left up the hill. Continue on a track to reach a farm, going to the right of a barn and then joining a concrete drive, a pond on the right, leading out to a road.

4 Turn left and soon go right up a track. Your path goes up the left side of a hedge. Go through a swing gate and turn right on a surfaced drive; when this swings right, keep onward over grass, continuing to climb with woodland on your right. At the brow of the hill in front of a white house, you reach a ride and turn left. At a junction of rides just before a car park, turn left. At the next junction of rides turn right to go back on yourself. At another ride go left, and then right through a kissing gate. Cross a field and go through a gate onto a road, which you cross slightly left.

5 Enter woodland and go downhill and to the left of a small pond. At the first junction of paths go left. You should now be going steeply downhill for a short distance, after which keep going forward, ignoring side paths, to eventually reach a T-junction with open land ahead. Go left here to eventually emerge on a lane with a large barn alongside.

6 Go ahead and turn right along a drive. Immediately before the house called Brambles, turn left along a track labelled footpath 32. Once over a stile, the track becomes a hedged path which goes right a little way before leading to another stile. Strike out across two fields to enter woodland and encounter a familiar signpost.

7 *(At this point, if you want to avoid duplicating part of your outward journey and would like to complete the slightly longer option, go straight to point 8)* Go right over the stile and along the right-hand edge of this and the left-hand edge of the next field to cross a stile on the left. Go right to maintain your direction, cross a stile, and, at the next field boundary, go diagonally left to a bridge about 40 yards from the right-hand side of the field. Go to the far left corner of the next field and straight up the middle of the one after. From here go diagonally right to a stile into a main road. Continue left along the verge and then cross between gates to a path which takes you to Horndon on the Hill. Turn left at the top to return to the Bell.

8 Continue onwards, *or, if you are taking the short option from point 2, turn right.* The path is not clear, but you should emerge on a field to walk up the edge with a strip of woodland on your right. At the end of the hedge, walk straight ahead and continue down the right-hand side of the hedge which you come to. Follow this round to the right and cross over to walk on the left side of a hedge. After ¼ mile turn left on a clear track across a field towards the A13.

A thatcher at work

9 After passing through metal gates turn right and walk parallel with the road, with a fence on your left. After about 200 yards, you will see a footpath sign directing you diagonally across the field and away from the road. If you line up accurately with the sign you will arrive at a bridge taking you into a patch of woodland. Just before reaching a field on the other side, turn right in front of a burnt tree. This path takes you to the field edge further on. From here you can take a clear path across a field and eventually reach a hedge on the right, which you follow to a stile. Cross the B1007 diagonally right to a stile and turn right to go up the edge of the field. At the top, continue ahead between narrow fences and a wall, which you will be glad to discover belongs to the Bell. Turn left to the car park.

Place of Interest

Lakeside, a massive shopping centre, is within 10 miles of Horndon on the Hill. It is signed off the A13 and open from 10 am to 10 pm on weekdays, 9 am to 7.30 pm on Saturday and 11 am to 5 pm on Sunday.

Date walk completed:

....

25

The Hoop

At over 300 feet above sea level, it is probably the highest village in Essex, and this short walk explores the local hills and valleys. Along the way we pass through pastures which have hardly changed over the last 100 years and explore an area of ancient woodland.

The Hoop is a popular, delightful, pub, which is especially busy at

Stock consists of a picturesque high street, four pubs, three churches, a small but well stocked supermarket, an off licence, a newsagent's, a barber's and an award-winning fish and chip shop.

weekends. It is as well to choose a fine day for your visit so that you can eat and drink in the extensive garden, which contains a sheltered area. There is a tiny bar which serves the garden, and in the summer there is a regular barbeque. The Hoop excels in providing an extensive range of beers which includes at least six different brews. Adnams and Mighty Oak are always available. The food is good and varied, with dishes such as cottage pie, grilled skate, braised steak and dumplings, and a wide choice of vegetables.

Distance: 3¾ miles

OS Explorer 175 Southend on Sea and Basildon, Brentwood and Billericay and just the edge of OS Explorer 183 Chelmsford and the Rodings
GR 692991

The walk is rarely level, but there is only one steep ascent and descent

Starting point: The Hoop has no car park, but there is road-parking along its frontage.

How to get there: Stock is on the B1007, which runs between the A12 (Chelmsford) and A129 (Billericay). The Hoop is on the main road.

Opening times are 11 am to 11 pm (noon to 10.30 pm on Sunday). Food is served from 11 am to 2.30 pm and from 6 pm to 9 pm, Monday to Thursday; 11 am to 9 pm on Friday and Saturday; and noon to 8 pm on Sunday.

Telephone: 01277 841137.

The Walk

1 Leave the pub and walk towards the village centre, passing to the left of the war memorial and keeping to a gravel path which feeds into a side road. At the end of this street, turn left past The Bear Inn. Immediately past the entrance to Tansly Cottage, turn right down a narrow path which passes the Roman Catholic church, in the grounds of which traces of the Roman occupation have been found. At the end of this path go through a metal kissing gate and turn right. Walk

down to a bridge and up through a wooden gate into a churchyard. Walk up past the medieval church of All Saints, through a car park and across the road.

2 Turn left and take a gravel path to the right of a wooden cased pump. At the lane go right, and, where this turns sharply right, follow a concrete signpost to take a path on the left which goes to the right of a garden fence. You emerge on the right-hand edge of a field and continue ahead over a stile and between hedges. Eventually the path swings round to join

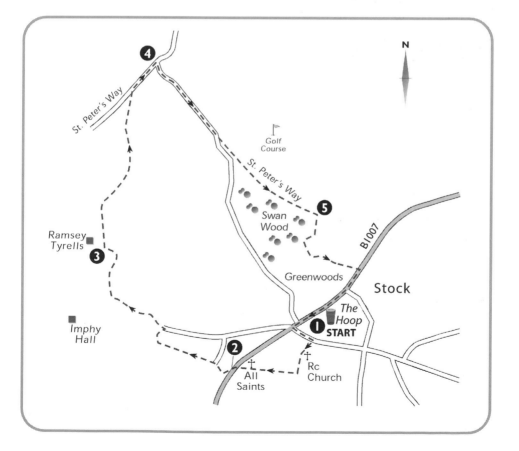

a track, which you follow to the right to join a lane, where you go left. The lane degenerates into a shingle track. Ignore the turning to Imphy Hall and keep with the track as it descends and then rises up to Ramsey Tyrrells Farm. Immediately after passing the first barn turn right.

All Saints' church, Stock

❸ Walk downhill over a cross-field path. Cross a stile and then walk up a meadow, following a line of telephone poles, and go along the left edge of the next field. Enter the final field of the sequence via a barrier and stile to reach a track and continue ahead for a few paces; then turn right up to an improvised gate into a field. From here go diagonally left to a stile in the far corner. Now turn right on a hedged track to reach a road.

❹ Turn right and follow the road for about ¼ mile. Look for a fingerpost on the left and enter the right-hand edge of a golf course. Keep to this path, which is generally well shielded from the course by young trees. Ignore a path to the right and eventually reach a bridge and an elaborate flight of steps to arrive on a lane by a brick house.

❺ Turn right to walk alongside a wood. Keep a lookout to the right for a gated path which is set back and leads into the wood; there is a Woodland Trust sign.

Follow the path, which goes downhill. At the bottom go left, ignoring a bridge on the right, and continue ahead on the lower of two paths, which gradually goes uphill. At the top, go right and walk just inside the edge and then rejoin the lane by a telephone mast. Passing Greenwoods Farm, follow the lane to the main road, which you cross; then turn right and walk along the pavement back to the Hoop.

Place of Interest
Hanningfield Reservoir is less than 2 miles from Stock. Walks in the area are, as yet, limited, but there is a grand visitor centre, a good picnic area, and access to hides for bird watching. Telephone: 01268 711001.

Date walk completed:
....

The Square and Compasses

Using good paths, this walk takes you beside and through woodland and along low ridges with attractive views. A visit to Terling provides the opportunity to see some ancient wall paintings in the church as well as some village architecture which just whets the appetite for what you will experience as you walk through charming Flack's Green.

At the **Square and Compasses**, carpenter's and woodman's tools are displayed together with corn dollies, stuffed birds and shooting pictures. This comfortable old pub has wood fires in winter and a welcoming garden in the summer. As this is a Ridley's house, you can depend on the quality of the ale. There is a long and attractive menu, which can include mussels, pork medallions, and grilled goat's cheese on pan-fried pears with balsamic vinegar, as well as sandwiches. The food is all home-cooked and is exceptionally good. This is a particularly friendly pub, to which you will want to return. Walkers wearing boots should use the tap room.

Opening times are 11.30 am to 3 pm and 6.30 pm (7 pm in winter) to 11 pm from Tuesday to Saturday, and from noon to 3 pm and 7 pm to 10.30 pm on Sunday. Bar Food is available from noon to 2.15 pm and from 7 pm to 9.30 pm (10 pm on Friday and Saturday). The pub is closed all day Monday except bank holidays.

Telephone: 01245 361477.

Distance: *5¼ miles*

OS Explorer 183 Chelmsford and the Rodings
GR 747161

Although there are lots of field-edge paths, this is a fairly dry walk with gentle inclines.

Starting point: The car park of the Square and Compasses. The licensees are pleased for you to park here as long as you give them your custom on your return.

How to get there: Fuller Street is most easily reached via Terling from Hatfield Peverel off the A12. It is also signposted from Little Waltham on the A130.

The Walk

1 Leave the pub car park and turn right to walk along the road signed to Rank's Green. Continue on this quiet lane for about ¼ mile. Go round the corner past Lodge Cottage and turn right by a concrete footpath sign to head towards Fairstead Lodge Farm. Continue ahead between farm buildings, passing silos on your right, and along the edge of a field, with the hedge and farmhouse on your left. The hedge gives way to a ditch, and you continue straight across a second field to cross a plank bridge and walk along the right-hand edge of Brickhouse Wood. Go to the right of a pylon and proceed along the left edge of the next (Hookley) wood. At its end, go through a gap but hold your direction, with the hedge on the left. Towards the end of the field you will arrive at a plantation of young trees: turn right and walk along its edge to reach a lane.

2 Turn left to walk up to Fairstead (the medieval church is worth visiting).

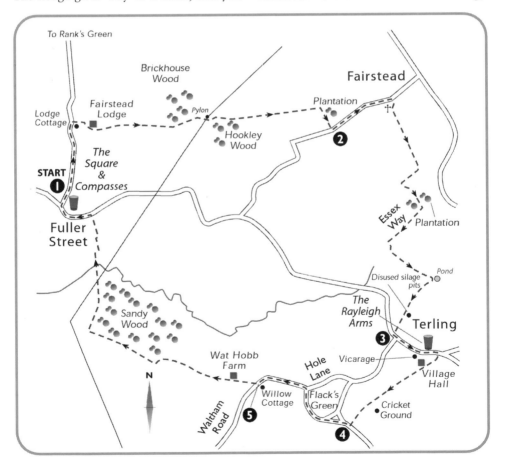

Immediately past the church, turn right onto the Essex Way and walk through a graveyard. Just before the end, turn right to cross a bridge and then left in front of a gate to walk down to a stile. Keep ahead across a field and climb three more stiles to continue up the middle of the next field on a broad track. At the field boundary turn right. Some 150 yards after passing the boundary of a wood, turn left over an earthen bridge and walk straight through to the other side. You should reach a plank bridge with a waymarker bearing the Essex Way logo (if not, walk along the side of the wood until you find it). From the bridge, go through a plantation and turn right at its boundary. Ignore a bridge on the left and continue until you reach another waymarker; here you turn left to follow the edge of a field. Almost immediately go through a gap on the right and turn left to continue up the hill with the hedge on your left. At the end of this field, turn right in front of a pond. Keep forward at the end of the hedge-line, passing disused silage pits on the left, to join a drive which brings you to a road.

3 Turn left along the road, passing the Old Vicarage. Just after passing the Rayleigh Arms and before a road junction, turn right and then right again, to walk along a wide drive with houses on your right. Soon you pass the village hall and then a series of other local amenities. Keep ahead at cross track and pass alongside a cricket ground. Continue, with a beech hedge on your right, until you reach a road.

4 Go right and then fork left. At the junction with Hole Lane, turn left along Waltham Road. On a corner opposite Willow Cottage turn right.

Approaching Fairstead

5 Pass a pond on the left. Once beyond a thatched cottage, the lane becomes a track. Cross stiles into and out of a field to join a wide path across a field and then walk along the left edge of Sandy Wood. Ignore two right turns. About 100 yards before power lines, turn right at a waymarker and continue downhill along the woodland edge, with power lines to the left. At the bottom of the hill, continue onwards to cross a bridge and walk up the right edge of a field to a waymarker. Turn right and then left to keep your direction, with the hedge now on your left. Turn left at the road and right at the junction to return to the Square and Compasses.

Place of Interest

Cressing Temple (GR 799188), can be reached via Rank's Green and White Notley. Here there are two barns once owned by the Knights Templar along with gardens and 17th century rural buildings. Opening times vary and so it is best to phone first: 01376 584903.

Date walk completed:

....

Great Yeldham

The White Hart

This is a short, easy walk offering brilliant views across the beautiful valley of the River Colne, one of the most attractive areas of Essex. Pleasant tree-lined paths connect the viewpoints, and, at the base of the valley, you cross a species-rich floodplain.

The White Hart, a grand low-beamed Tudor pub, is famed for its dining experience; so you can expect fine food and would be well advised to book in advance if you intend to eat in the restaurant, especially at weekends. The food in the bar and in the restaurant is not cheap, but is of superb quality. It ranges from sandwiches to dishes like calves liver with bubble and squeak, crispy bacon and honey roast parsnips. There is a good range of real ales, with Adnams always on tap.

Opening times are 11 am to 11 pm every day (noon start on Sunday). Food is served from noon to 2 pm and from 6.30 pm to 9.30 pm.

Telephone: 01787 237250.

Distance: 3½ miles

OS Explorer 195 Braintree and Saffron Walden
GR 762377

There is one noticeable climb, but most of the gradients are very gentle. The paths are generally in good condition all year round, although there is a stretch near the start of point three which can get quite muddy.

Starting point: The White Hart car park. The landlord is quite happy for you to use the pub car park whilst you walk, as long as you park at right angles to the pub and give him your custom on your return.

How to get there: The White Hart is at the southern end of Great Yeldham on the A1017, about halfway between Haverhill and Braintree.

The Walk

① Leave the pub car park, cross the road, and turn left to walk up to the junction. Go left along the road signed to Toppesfield. You'll pass a Strict Baptist chapel on the left and an industrial estate on the right before entering a residential area. At a concrete road on the right, immediately before a house called Redruth, turn right and go through a metal barrier into playing fields. Then walk diagonally left to pick up a path by a fence, which takes you behind a pavilion. Follow the tree-lined path into a field, with a good view of the rather grand Great Yeldham church over to the right.

② Go on a few steps and then go left along a field edge, with a ditch on your right. Follow this field edge for the best part of a mile as it twists and turns, ignoring a path going off to the right. (On a clear day you will have views for miles to left and right.) When you reach the end of the field, go right over a plank bridge by a waymarker. Now go left along the edge of the next field and go left through a gap at the field corner onto a lane.

③ Turn left. After passing a bungalow, the lane deteriorates into a track. (The early part of this track can become very boggy at wet times of the year. Further on it dries out and becomes a very pleasant trail with trees arching over and many inquisitive birds flitting in and out.) You will come to a bridge with a metal rail, which takes you into a field; here you go left, following the edge and passing Scotneys Croft to reach a road.

④ Cross over and go left and almost immediately right by a fingerpost, passing the entrance to a house; go down a track. This soon swings left, but carry straight on down another tree-edged path, soon joining another track swinging right and

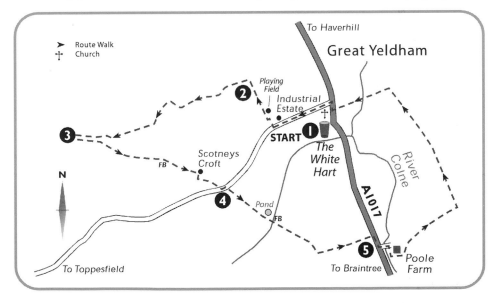

left to pass a large pond on your left. Past the pond, join a narrow path to a bridge across a stream and go straight across its floodplain. Cross a stile and keep ahead to climb up the other side of the valley. (On the ground you may see the small, deeply indented tracks of the muntjak deer, a very small deer of Asiatic origin, which from a distance could be mistaken for a dog.) At the top of the rise, walk

Morning mist on the Colne Valley

through a gap in the hedge at a waymarker and then left on another sheltered track, which takes you to a road.

5 Cross over and turn right. Turn left, crossing a bridge over the River Colne to the main entrance of Poole Farm. Unless you are visiting the farm shop, turn right in front of the farm buildings. (Notice the fancy brickwork on the old industrial building.) Walk to the end and here turn left to join a broad track going uphill. Over on your right you will see Castle Hedingham. When you reach a waymarker just before trees on the right, go left across the field to reach a hedge corner, turning right into the field and then left, to walk with the hedge on your left. In this area you will see the tracks of the much larger fallow deer. (I didn't actually see any when I was there, but I did see a stoat, a much rarer sighting.) Walk up the side of a wood and then, in a second field, go slightly left across the centre and cross over a stream. Then cross the next field. At the top go through a metal kissing gate and then turn left onto a good track downhill, recrossing the Colne and arriving at the road. Turn left to return to the White Hart.

Date walk completed:

....

Place of Interest

Colne Valley Railway lies about a mile and a half down the road (south) from your starting point. It uses about a mile of restored track and has a station, rolling stock, and artefacts of general interest. It incorporates the **Colne Valley Farm Park**, which in addition to its traditional farm animals offers a wealth of wild flora and fauna. Telephone: 01787 461174.

the remarkable village of Castle Hedingham.

Once you have climbed out of the town and had the first tantalizing glimpse of the local castle, the outward journey is mainly over arable country with wide views. Near Gestingthorpe you enter an area exhibiting a rich diversity of flora. The return is along wide grassy tracks, to eventually zigzag your way through the village and past the magnificent brick-built church.

The major problem you are likely to have with this walk is actually dragging yourself away from the small network of streets, lined with wonderful terraces of houses interspersed with grander mansions, which make up

Distance: 5½ miles

OS Explorer 195 Braintree and Saffron Walden
GR 786356

A fairly level walk with just one challenging stile.

Starting point: The car park of the Bell, but please ask first just in case they have a reception booked. (If this is the case there is generally ample parking space along the road or behind the church.)

How to get there: The village is situated on the B1058, a short distance off the A1017, about halfway between Haverhill and Braintree.

The Bell is a wonderful old coaching house which has resisted any tampering over the years. It has a honeycomb of rooms, all with separate fires, and a vast garden for summer drinking. The beers are served direct from the cask and include a beautiful mild, Oscar Wilde. A good range of home-cooked and reasonably priced food includes standards like steak and ale pudding as well as more exotic Thai and Turkish dishes.

Time your visit to the last Sunday lunchtime of the month and you will be entertained by a traditional jazz group.

Opening times are from 11.30 am to 3 pm and 6 pm to 11 pm, Monday to Saturday, and from noon to 4 pm and 7 pm to 10.30 pm on Sunday.

Telephone: 01787 460 350.

The Walk

1 From the Bell, turn left along St James Street and into Queen's Street; go left along Pottery Lane and right along a narrow footpath. Climb some steps and turn left through two squeeze stiles and continue to a concrete path which swings right to reach a road on a small estate. Turn left and then right to go uphill on an asphalt path which quickly changes into a grassy track. At the top, turn left with the field edge (you will have your first sight of the castle over to the left). Look for a telegraph pole near the path; here turn right on a path that crosses the field, passing a solitary oak, and goes down to a rather precarious stile, which you cross to turn left and reach a lane.

2 Turn right and walk towards Little Lodge Farm. Go left before the farm, passing between buildings to go through a hedge and turn right before soon turning left onto a path across a field. At the end of the field go right for a few yards and

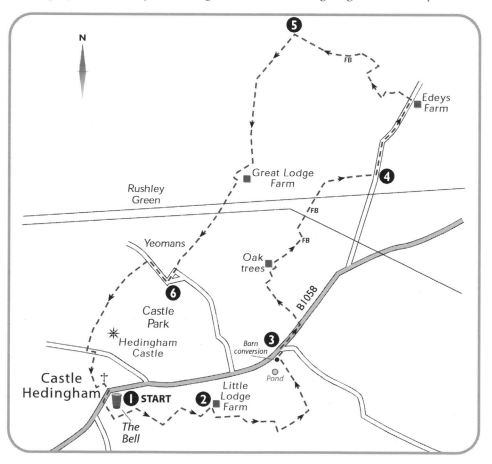

then left to continue across the next field in your previous direction. Join a byway for a short distance before going left on another cross-field path, passing to the right of a pond surrounded by trees and turning right in front of some barn conversions. Emerge at a road junction.

3 Take the far road signed to Gestingthorpe. At a break in the line of the trees, go left along a path on the field edge. (In fact, when I was here, the farmer had left a track about 4 yards from the field edge in this and the following fields, which was much more convenient to walk on.) The path follows the remnants of a ditch and a hedge. When confronted with a solid hedge, go right and then left to reach a small block of older oak trees, at the end of which you go left. Then turn right to walk with a ditch on your right to the field corner; here you cross a bridge and turn left. At a waymarker go right up the edge of the field with a ditch on the left, passing under power lines. Go right for a few yards before going left over a plank bridge through the hedge. Go towards a further set of power lines, and, after going round a pylon, continue across the field at the next waymarker, stepping over a low fence into a lane.

4 Turn left and follow this charming lane (which in spring and summer is full of wild flowers) to reach Edeys Farm; fork left onto a rougher track. After about 200 yards, just before a bend, go left up the right edge of the field. Keep with the hedge as it goes round to the right and cross a bridge up the edge of the next field to curve to the left along the line of a wood. Cross a bridge with a metal handrail to join a wide track going right and immediately take a left fork and walk

along a line of isolated oaks to reach a waymarker.

5 Turn left along a field edge. Keep on this wide grassy track as it eventually swings left towards farm buildings. As you approach, ignore the bridge on your left to follow the track around to the right of Great Lodge Farm. Go under power lines and join a concrete drive which after about $1/_3$ mile feeds into a lane. When you reach a triangle of trees and grass go right on a path to reach the road.

6 Go right and, later, cross a stile opposite a house called Yeomans. Go downhill on the right-hand side of a small valley, crossing a stile at the bottom to join a tree-lined lane. (From here you can see part of the castle beyond the visitors' car park.) When you reach the road, cross over and turn left and then right along Crown Street. Fork right up Church Lane and climb the steps on the left into the churchyard. Leave by the war memorial and go right up King Street and left along St James Street to return to the Bell.

Place of Interest

You may have been disappointed at the way your view of **Hedingham Castle** was obscured by the trees and it would be a shame to leave the village without visiting this remarkably well preserved Norman keep. It has four floors, which include a banqueting hall and minstrels' gallery, in addition to extensive grounds. Telephone: 01787 460261.

Date walk completed:

....

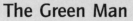

The Green Man

This is a walk for nature lovers as it has an interesting array of fauna and flora. The start features a

Distance: *5 miles*

OS Explorer 195 Braintree and Saffron Walden
GR 784295

A walk mainly on good paths; there are a few gentle inclines

Starting point: You are welcome to leave your car in the pub car park, either before or after using their facilities, but please ask first. There is additional parking opposite in The Limes.

How to get there: Gosfield is at the southern end of the A1017, which runs between Haverhill and Braintree. The Green Man is on the main road, The Street, to the south of the village.

circuit amongst the ponds of Sandpits Nature Reserve before striking out to Broak's Wood with its mix of ancient woodland and coniferous trees. On the return you will pass alongside an abandoned airfield which has been replanted with trees and has a feast of meadow flowers – it is here that you are likely to see deer crossing the wide track. The return to Gosfield passes through the grounds of the church and eventually along The Street where mixed housing dates back to medieval times.

The Green Man is famous locally for its weekday cold table, which features home-cooked ham, turkey, tongue and beef together with game pie, poached and smoked salmon, and a whole range of pickles and salads. Good traditional bar food is also available as are cask ales. This is a very popular dining pub and it is as well to book, even during the week.

Opening times are 11 am to 2.30 pm and 6.30 pm to 11 pm, Monday to Saturday, and noon to 2.30 pm and 7 pm to 10.30 pm on Sunday. No food is served on Sunday evening.

Telephone: 01787 472746.

The Walk

1 On leaving the Green Man, turn right and walk as far as the King's Head. Opposite the pub, turn right along a gravel drive, which leads to a green barrier, on through a corridor of woodland and through another barrier to enter Sandpits Nature Reserve. At the first junction of paths, go right, with a pond on your left. Go left at a fork and cross a slatted bridge. Now keep ahead, ignoring side paths. Soon you will pass more ponds on the left. The path then swings left to reach a T-junction with a lake ahead. Turn right to go up and then down steps passing between two large ponds. At the next T-junction turn left and keep to this path to emerge on a stony track which bears left across a clearing.

2 Go right through a barrier and along a wide track. Just before a gate, turn right and walk just inside woodland down to a bridge and stile. Cross the field by the path and continue onwards, with a hedge on your left, to reach a lane.

3 Turn left. At the junction with the main road, turn right and pass an entrance to Gosfield School. After about 250 yards and opposite cottage number 3,

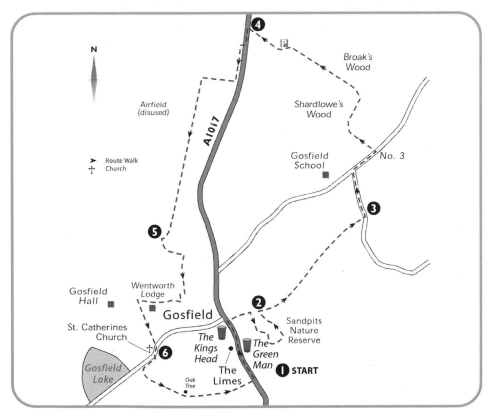

39

cross over and walk along the edge of the woodland. At the first junction of paths go right. Keep to this path, which can be very muddy at times, until you come to an obvious cross-track; here you turn left. Soon the path joins a more substantial track coming in from the right; you follow this for nearly ½ mile until you come to a gate leading into a car parking and picnic area. Continue onwards, passing a couple of small ponds on your right, to eventually reach a road.

In the Sandpits Nature Reserve

❹ Cross over the road and turn left, looking for a track entrance on the right; go into this, but, immediately before the gate, turn left so that you are now walking along a narrow fenced path which runs parallel to the road. Keep with the path as it proceeds unfenced along the edge of a second field. Towards the end the path swings right, so that you are walking with a hedge on your left towards what appears to be a large television receiver dish mounted on a pole. On reaching a concrete area, turn left through a gate to walk along one of the service roads of the old airfield. Follow this track for nearly ¾ mile. Eventually it curves right, and you follow the hedge on the left until it ends.

❺ Turn left to walk along the field edge. The path soon swaps sides with the hedge; so you find yourself walking with the hedge on your right. After 150 yards, turn right at a waymarker to join a narrow path along the backs of gardens. You eventually emerge on a drive and turn right, passing Wentworth Lodge on the left. Just before reaching some white gates ahead, swing left onto a path crossing a field towards Gosfield church and a road.

❻ Cross the road and go right for a few

yards to join a footpath which runs inside the hedge parallel to the road. Walk to the end of the field and follow the hedge to the left as it hugs the field edge. When the hedge is replaced by a wooden fence, go straight on, to the right of a lonely oak in the middle of the field. Now go slightly left past a partly hedged sewage works and walk down to a stile onto a lane. Turn left up the lane. Just before gates and the road, veer left to a stile and turn left to return to the starting point.

Places of Interest

Gosfield Lake Resort, just to the west of the village, is a private, family-run leisure park, with shops, eating places and a play area (open April to October). Telephone: 01787 475043.

Gosfield Hall, originally a two-storey brick courtyard house, was built in 1545 by Sir John Wentworth. It was extensively remodelled in the late 17th century. The main rooms and gardens are open to the public Telephone: 01787 472 914.

Date walk completed:

....

The Prince of Wales

This is very much a walk of two parts. The outward route is straightforward, allowing plenty of time for uninterrupted contemplation of the extensive views over the Crouch and Blackwater valleys. The return trip has more variety, crossing arable land and pasture linked by interesting hedged paths.

Along the way you will pass through Purleigh and Cold Norton and see the remains of the best-preserved First World War airfield in Britain. The churches are particularly interesting. Purleigh church was once the living of George Washington's great-great grandfather, the Reverend Lawrence Washington, who was removed from office for consuming too much of the local brew. On the spire of Stow Maries church is an incongruous illuminated cross, erected by a former wing commander of the airfield in 1931. It is claimed to be the precursor of the illuminated advertising in Piccadilly Circus!

The Prince of Wales is a surprisingly lively pub to find in such a quiet, out-of-the-way village. It seems to have special events, including fish nights and beer festivals, almost every week. The food is very good and quite reasonably priced. Fish (and unusual fish at that) is a speciality, whilst the range of about five real ales is sure to include at least of couple that you are unlikely to have heard of before.

Opening times are from 11 am to 11 pm, Monday to Saturday, and noon to 10.30 pm on Sunday. Food is served from noon to 2.30 pm and from 7 pm to 9.30 pm, and from noon to 9.30 pm on Sunday.

Telephone: 01621 828971.

Distance: *7 miles*

OS Explorer 175 Southend on Sea and Basildon, 183 Chelmsford and The Rodings GR 830995

It starts with a bit of a climb but becomes a straightforward walk along field edges

Starting point: The car park of the Prince of Wales, with the landlord's permission.

How to get there: Stow Maries is most easily approached by going north off the B1010, just east of South Woodham Ferrers.

The Walk

1 Leave the car park of the Prince of Wales and walk left across the front to turn left at the end of its boundary and walk ahead. Once past the patch of scrub on the left, turn sharp left to cross a stile onto a fenced path and continue over another. After crossing a stile into a field, go slightly right and then left up the right-hand edge of a field. Keep on to the top of the field and then keep with the edge as the hedge goes left. The hedge swings right and then left; now look for a gap in the hedge down to a stile (it is about 40 yards along; if you come to too large a gap, you have gone too far).

2 You are now walking along the fence on the left side of a long field. (To the left is the mess hut and office of a First World War airfield.) After about ½ mile, just past Flambirds Farm, you come to the first field boundary, which you cross by a bridge. After two more fields you cross a concrete track, and then pass the mounds of reservoirs on the right. You now enter the final field of the sequence, on a wide, mown, grass path. Keep to the left edge to reach a road.

3 Cross and go

ahead over a complex of cross-tracks to walk along the right hedge of a field; there is a power line going off diagonally on your left. (You are now on St Peter's Way, the 43-mile path from Chipping Ongar to Bradwell.) At the end of the hedge, go straight across the field; at its boundary, turn right and keep with the hedge as it turns left to reach a road.

4 Turn right then left at the junction and pass Scott's Farm. After ¼ mile, immediately after a 30 mph sign, turn right down a stony track. In front of Brookwood this swings right and degenerates into a rather muddier version as it resumes its original

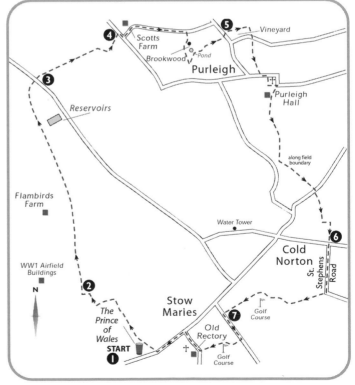

42

direction. Near the top of a rise, cross a stile on the left and go alongside a barn. Then head for the far left corner of the field, where another stile delivers you into a tunnel of scrub. Go right and immediately left, passing a small pond. Now follow the path as it descends through scrub, ignoring a fork to the right.

5 Go diagonally left at the road, cross a plank bridge and go through a vineyard. At a concrete path turn right and go straight across the road, through a metal gate and up the middle of a field to the protruding corner of a hedge. Continue, with this on your right, into the far corner through a piece of land which is usually uncultivated, reaching a stile which takes you down into the road. Turn left and then right to enter the grounds of Purleigh church. Leave by a yew avenue, turn right and walk towards Purleigh Hall. Continue ahead and cross a stile. Walk near the upper edge of one field and enter a second via a double stile. Go slightly left and cross to the nearest trees; here, by a fallen tree-trunk, you will discover a bridge leading to a superb hedged path. When you reach a field go left; then go left through a gap and right along the field boundary unless the farmer has left a path veering slightly left up the field. Cross the stream by an earthen bridge and go slightly left up the hill to an obvious gap. On reaching a wide track, turn right and soon cross a stile with a waymarker on your left. Walk ahead, gradually joining the hedge on your left; on reaching the far left-hand corner, proceed with a hedge on your right. Cross one more stile and turn left when you reach open land. Cross the field to a stile which takes you into a lane. Turn right.

6 Cross the main road at Cold Norton and walk down St Stephen's Road. Where this curves left, leave it. Go past a metal gate and right along the edge of a golf course; short green posts indicate the way. When the hedge ends, cross a fairway and walk alongside another hedge with a ditch on the left. A line of posts now takes you forward to the right of a pond. At the post just before the pond, turn right to another post in front of an oak tree. Continue with a hedge on your right to reach a gravel track, on which you turn left and walk to a narrow lane.

7 Turn left. After ¼ mile, turn right onto another golf course. Go ahead to a waymarker. Three more markers take you right, left, and right again, so that you eventually walk up the right-hand side of the course to emerge, between fences, on a lane in front of the impressive Old Rectory. Turn right and pass the church with the illuminated cross; then turn left at the main road to reach the Prince of Wales.

Place of Interest
Marsh Farm Country Park, to the south of South Woodham Ferrers, is open at weekends, and during the week from February to October. Here you can follow farm trails featuring a whole range of domesticated animals besides watching daily milking operations. There's also a gift shop, tearoom and play area. Telephone: 01245 324191.

Date walk completed:
....

many species of waders in vast numbers on your left, as well as game birds and at least three varieties of geese to the right.

The return, over good tracks, will give you the chance to see the separate hamlets of Paglesham and to wonder why they are not connected by a more direct route.

Wrap up well and take your binoculars!

Although interesting all the year round, I would save this walk up for one of those crisp, bright, clear autumn mornings when the tide is going out. The walk along the River Roach will provide plenty of opportunity to view

The name **Plough & Sail** nicely conjures up what once must have been the mix of clientele at this pub. You won't see many farmers here now, but there are plenty of boat-owners with vessels in the yards around the corner. This is a 400-year-old white-painted weather-boarded pub. Outside, there's a leafy garden with trestle tables, an aviary, and children's play area. Inside, you have the usual pub furniture relieved by an open brick fireplace, horse brasses, copper kettles and ship's lanterns. There is generally a good range of fresh fish dishes as well as choices from the cold cabinet. In addition, there is a good range of traditional bar food, including sandwiches. The beer is Greene King. It is a popular place, especially at weekends, and you are advised to book.

Distance: 5½ miles

OS Explorer 176 Blackwater Estuary, Maldon, Burnham-on-Crouch and Southend-on-Sea
GR 943924

This is an extremely easy walk to follow and the paths are generally good.

Starting point: The car park of the Plough & Sail, but be sure to ask permission first.

How to get there: It is probably best to aim for Rochford first. Once there, take the road east signed to Ballard's Gore. Paglesham is signed from here, but be sure to keep right to avoid going out to Church End

Opening times from Monday to Saturday are from noon to 3 pm (11.30 am to 3.30 pm on Saturday) and 6.30 pm to 11 pm. Sunday opening is from noon to 11 pm.

Telephone: 01702 258242.

The Walk

1 Leave the car park and turn right. Go right again down by the side of the pub on an unmade road towards Essex Boatyards. Follow the track as it swings right along the front of Cobblers Row and continue along it until you reach the actual boatyard. Go diagonally right to the central barrier and walk forward to reach the sea wall. (Here you will pass between fabulous boats of all descriptions.) Look for a slipway with brick steps to the right and go up them to start walking south-west along the wall. (You will be following this easy path along the River Roach for just over 2½ miles; so you will have plenty of opportunity to observe the thousands of birds which cluster on the mud flats and inland at particular times of the year. In the early autumn you can collect plenty of mushrooms, field and parasol, for your tea (make sure that you check them first).) Just after Stannets Creek, you will pass a large lake. After this, you are tracked by a large drainage ditch on the right until you reach a Second World War pillbox at Finches.

2 From here the path veers away from the river, following, at a distance, the route of Bartonhall Creek. Keep following the wall supporting the path as it gets lower and lower until it is soon only a foot or two above the adjoining ground. Eventually it comes to a dead end at a thicket of trees. Turn right, cross carefully a usually overgrown plank bridge, scramble up a small bank and go left on a farm track.

3 Follow the track as it swings right; at a T-junction, go right and then soon left up the edge of a large field. After ¼ mile, swing right with the track to continue following the field boundary (ahead you should see the lake). Soon the first waymarker of the day guides you

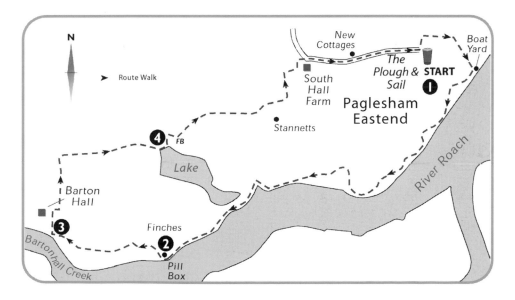

through a very pleasant tree-lined section. When you emerge you will be walking along the left-hand side of the hedge. (Now is the time to get your camera ready for a photo opportunity, because, as you reach the lake you are likely to disturb a whole flock of birds.)

④ From the lake, turn left. After a few yards, by another waymarker, take the middle of three paths and descend from the bank. At the bottom go diagonally right to cross a dip then go left to walk up a bank, along the edge of a field with a ditch on your left. Eventually, you join a tree-lined track, which can be muddy. Pass a metal gate and follow the track until you come to South Hall Farm. Turn

The parasol mushroom

left in front of a large barn, and, at its end, turn right to reach the road. Go right along the road for about ½ mile to return to the Plough and Sail.

Date walk completed:

....

Place of Interest

It is hard to believe, given the isolated nature of the Paglesham hamlets, that you are less than ten miles from **Southend**. If you have the energy you could consider walking the 1.33 miles along the longest pier in the world. Otherwise you can settle for the pier museum and lifeboat. Telephone: 01702 215620.

Fingringhoe 14 `Walk`
The Whalebone

On the outward journey on this delightful walk, you travel along one of the most attractive byways in Essex and then cross the Roman river to enter Ministry of Defence land at Donyland Woods (*see note at beginning of walk directions*). This mixed woodland with well defined paths is reason enough for your outing, but there is much more to come. You walk down through trees and beside a lake into Rowhedge, passing its extraordinary church, to reach the quayside, with panoramic views across the River Colne to Wivenhoe. Now you have a chance to see the waders on the mudflats as you return via an old tidal mill to the quiet village of Fingringhoe.

The Whalebone is a wonderful pub. You are welcomed into a simple but attractive interior with plain floorboards and stripped pine furniture, warmed by an open fire in winter. This is a free house, and the four beers on tap regularly change but you are likely to find well kept Greene King IPA and such treats as Archer's and Young's. The food is quite superb, with dishes such as cherry tomato and goat's cheese tart tartin, and pork and chestnut sausage with mashed potato, mustard and gravy. If you prefer a snack, freshly toasted ciabattas come in about eight varieties.

Opening times all week are 10 am to 3 pm and 5.30 pm to 11 pm. In summer, the pub is open all day on Saturday and Sunday, from 10 am to 11 pm.

Telephone: 01206 729307.

Distance: 4½ miles

OS Explorer 184 Colchester, Harwich and Clacton-on-Sea
GR 028204

A walk through woods, along byways and rivers. Gradients are slight, and the four stiles are all at the end.

Starting point: The pub car park. The licensee is happy for you to use the pub car park whilst you are walking, but please seek permission.

How to get there: Fingringhoe is signed off the A134, south of Colchester. As you approach the village, cross a bridge over the Roman river and the pub is on the right.

The Walk

Note: As the route goes through Middlewick firing range at point 3, you need to check that it is not being used for practice on the day of your intended walk. Warning flags are flown at both ends of the path but you can find out beforehand by phoning 01206 735203 or 736012 or 783206.

❶ Leave the pub and turn right. Walk along the road for about ¼ mile to reach a small green with a village sign. Turn right to walk down a lane, passing West House Farm. Soon the lane is hedged on both sides. Just over halfway along this byway

you will pass the rather attractive but dilapidated Upper Hay Farm. The lane ends at a road.

❷ Turn right along Hay Lane. At a T-junction with the B1025, go right and cross the Roman river. After about 200 yards, enter a lay-by on the right.

❸ Almost immediately turn right at a fingerpost. You are entering an area used by the Ministry of Defence for training, so there are warning notices as you pass the white gates and start up a clear stony track. Continue on the main track and avoid any diversions, however attractive they may seem. About halfway along, you

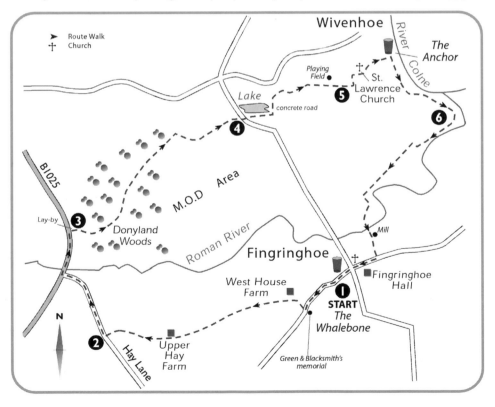

will descend to cross what remains of a stream by an earthen bridge and climb up the other side. Keep ahead, going slightly left at a prominent fork, then right at a major junction of tracks, with large trees. Swing left to come to a wide cross-track, with boggy ground to the right. Turn right, go left at a T-junction and continue ahead to a kissing gate which leads to a road.

Wivenhoe from across the Colne river

4 Cross to a footpath alongside and above a lake, at the end of which you turn left by your first waymarker of the day. Cross a concrete road to walk along the backs of houses and turn right at a second waymarker. You are now on the outskirts of Rowhedge and will emerge on a playing field; here go ahead, with a line of trees on your left.

5 Leave the playing fields and walk down a road; go left at the first junction and then take the second turning on the right to reach St Lawrence's church. Go through the churchyard and continue walking downhill, turning right in front of the Anchor public house on Rowhedge quay. Turn right to walk alongside the River Colne. At a large works car park, turn left, with a concrete wall and superior kitchen garden on your left. You will be led by arrows along the left perimeter of the industrial site. Soon the junction of the Colne with the Roman river is reached.

6 Swing right around the industrial site on a flood bank. Where the factory buildings end the path divides. Take the right fork with a wooden fence. Go down steps into a wooded area and go left to join a path, indicated by a fingerpost, which passes through young trees and scrub and then bears off, slightly left, along a hedgeline with open grassland on the right. When the hedge ends, keep straight ahead and go down through more trees. Cross a plank bridge and go up some steps. Ignore a stile on the right and continue in the direction of the mill on the bank to a bridge and stile. Cross a field to another stile and steps leading up to an asphalt path over the river, with the mill on your right. In the 16th century, this was a tidal mill with a wheel underneath, but it was converted to steam in the 1800s. Continue uphill to reach the road, where you turn right, and, passing Fingringhoe Hall on the left and the church on the right, return to the Whalebone.

Date walk completed:

....

Place of Interest

Nearby **Colchester** has many attractions. The **Castle Museum** is in the largest Norman keep in Europe with extensive displays of the town's Roman past and its role in the Civil War. Telephone: 01206 282939.

The Red Lion

This area is part of the Brecks, a tract of light sandy soil, much of which is given over to forestry. Half of this walk is along the bank of the River Lark, which flows westward from Bury St Edmunds to join the Great Ouse river near Ely. The return is through forest and across farmland.

Distance: 6¾ miles or 6 miles from the alternative start

OS Explorer 226 Ely & Newmarket and 229 Thetford Forest in The Brecks GR 771729/765732

An easy, level walk

Starting point: The Red Lion, Icklingham. If leaving your car, please check with the landlord first. Alternatively, start from point 2, 300 yards along the minor road from its junction with the A1101, where vehicles are prohibited. There is room for some cars on the minor road nearby.

How to get there: Icklingham is on the A1101 road between Bury St Edmunds and Mildenhall. The Red Lion is on the south side of the road near the western end of the village.

The **Red Lion**, a 16th-century inn, is an imposing building, standing well back from the road behind a wide lawn and commodious car park. The dining area extends over three rooms, and there are some large tables suitable for parties of 7 or 8. The Red Lion serves traditional English food with interesting accompaniments and fresh vegetables. For example, there is gammon and mustard sauce, and Barnsley lamb chops with mint and butter. You will not find chips anywhere. Interesting fish dishes are also available, such as whole grilled red gurnard with tomato and garlic butter.

Opening times are from noon to 2.30 pm and from 6.15 pm to 10 pm (7 pm to 9 pm on Sunday evening).

Telephone: 01638 717802.

The Walk

1 From the Red Lion, go left along the road, passing St James's church on the left. Ignore a road to a mill on the left, and just by the flint-faced old school, now a community centre, bear left along a minor road, passing Temple Close on the right.

2 Come to a turning space. The road beyond is prohibited to motor vehicles. Walk on along the road, which gradually changes to a gravel track. In about quarter of a mile, the track bends left, and, in a further quarter mile reaches Temple bridge over the River Lark.

3 Do not cross, but, immediately before the bridge, turn right along a cart track, very soon passing a stream gauging station. Continue along a grass path following the River Lark on the left. The footpath is part of the Lark Valley Path

that runs from Bury St Edmunds to Mildenhall. Continue along the river bank for about 1½ miles.

4 On reaching the corner of a mature wood on the right, leave the Lark Valley Path at a waymark, turning right over a sleeper bridge and continue just inside the wood. Cross a timber bridge with handrails and follow the footpath through the mixed woodland to reach the A1101 Bury to Mildenhall road. Carefully cross the main road and turn left along it. In 50 yards, turn right, and, passing beside a steel barrier gate, enter the forest along a grassy forest ride. Ahead, about 300 yards away, you will see the traffic on the A11 main road.

5 About halfway along the ride, turn right at a right-angled intersection with another forest ride. Soon pass an uncultivated area on the left and later

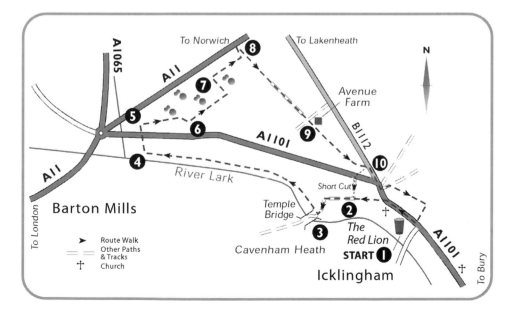

continue with mature trees on both sides. The forest ride ends at a T-junction; here go right for about 10 yards, and then turn left.

❻ Ignoring a stile into a field straight ahead, swing slightly left and follow a narrower grass path between the edge of the forest plantation on the left and a fence on the right. Eventually, where the grass path ends, turn left along a ride between stands of conifers.

❼ In a little over 200 yards, turn right onto another ride. When you reach the fence at the edge of the forest, follow the path round to the left, roughly under some electricity wires, and soon leave the forest, passing a steel barrier gate. Swing right a little to meet a hard track coming from the A11.

❽ Turn right, and, after passing a few old pine trees on the left, continue along a broad grass way between fields, with a row of widely spaced pines on the left. At the corner of a stand of conifers, keep straight on along a cart track, with the wood on the right. Where the trees on the right end, pass a track coming in from the left and keep straight on, reaching flint-faced Avenue Farm Cottages in about half a mile.

❾ Here leave the cart track and go straight on along a grass path, passing the end of the cottages about 20 yards to the right. Your path winds through a wooded area and soon comes out to the corner of a large field. Keep along the headland, passing another row of widely spaced mature pine trees and arriving at a road.

❿ (For the shorter walk, turn right, away

Temple bridge over the River Lark

from the road, along a broad grass path at the edge of an open area of grass, walking towards some houses. On reaching a road, cross over and continue along a lane that will bring you back to the end of the road where the motor vehicle prohibition signs are.) Otherwise, go right along the road to reach reach the A1101 in 200 yards and turn left. In 50 yards come to a junction with a private drive at a grassy triangle. At the end of the triangle turn left along a gravelly byway and almost immediately loop round right to pick up a lane between hedges. In quarter of a mile, turn right along a narrow path beside a fence on the left. Walk to the road and turn right to go back to the Red Lion.

Place of Interest
At **West Stow Country Park**, about 3 miles to the East of Icklingham, there is a reconstructed Anglo-Saxon village, a museum, café and visitor centre. Telephone: 01284 728718.

Date walk completed:

....

The Black Lion

Long Melford, besides having a long, wide and attractive village street, can boast two Elizabethan stately homes: Melford Hall and Kentwell Hall. On a slight hill, Holy Trinity church, built in the Perpendicular style, dominates the scene. The walk, partly along the route of the Stour Valley Path, starts near the church, passes Kentwell Hall, and circles through farmland to end opposite the gatehouse of Melford Hall.

It is said that there has been a **Black Lion** on the site overlooking Long Melford Green since 1661. This is a welcoming establishment, now a hotel. Meals are served in its well-appointed dining room or at tables outside. Far from run-of-the-mill, the menu serves interesting fare such as sea bass fillets with roasted fennel and pernod sauce, and leek, mushroom and fetta cheese pudding with roasted vegetables. However, the inclusion of Long Melford sausages and mash also ensures that local favourites are not forgotten. The ales served include Adnams and Nethergate.

Distance: *5 miles*

OS Explorer 196 Sudbury, Hadleigh and Dedham Vale
GR 865466

A walk on well-defined paths

Starting point: The Black Lion, Church Lane. There is a limited amount of parking along Church Lane between the Black Lion and the church.

How to get there: Long Melford is about 3 miles north of Sudbury, just off the A134 (Sudbury to Bury) road that bypasses the village. The Black Lion is near the church, at the northern end of the village.

Opening times are from noon to 2 pm at lunchtime and from 7 pm til late in the evening.

Telephone: 01787 312356.

The Walk

1 Walk up the road towards Holy Trinity church and enter the churchyard. Follow the gravel path round to the left of the tower and leave the churchyard through a gate to the Rectory. Where the drive bends right, go straight on, over a stile, into pasture. In about 50 yards, turn right through a squeeze stile and cross a field to another squeeze stile to enter a small wood. Leave the wood at

another stile and go straight on, as waymarked, across Kentwell Park. Some 150 yards from the wood, the path bends slightly to the right. At the far side of the field, cross a stile and meet the limetree avenue that leads to Kentwell Hall.

2 Turn left and walk along the drive. Immediately before an entrance gate/barrier, turn left, as signed, along a gravel track and through a gate and then a small wood. Continue along the track

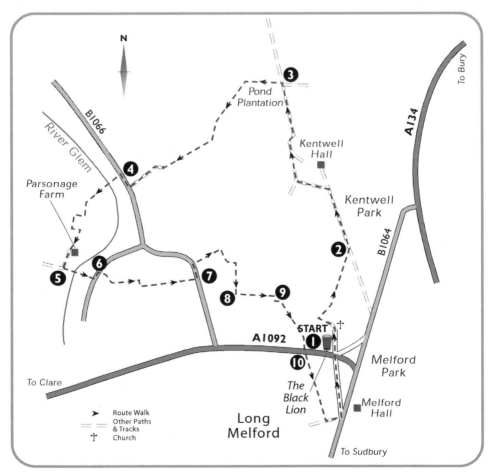

The summer house at Melford Hall

beside a fence on the left with Kentwell Hall a field away on the right. Immediately before a gateway, turn right beside a hedge and walk through a pasture field; at the corner, pass through a squeeze stile to a gravel drive. Go straight on, at first between hedges.

3 At a point where a similar track joins from the right, turn left beside a wood along a broad grassy headland path (there is a four-way signpost here). Go through a field boundary. Soon, where the wood on the left ends, keep straight on. About 100 yards beyond the wood, look out for a waymark and turn half right along a path across a field. At the far side of the field, cross a timber bridge and continue through some rough grassland. At the approach to some farm buildings, join a sandy track and swing left to walk through a yard between sheds; continue to the road. Here turn right and in about 200 yards pass on the left a flint-faced building.

4 At the corner of the building, and immediately before yellow Mill Farm, turn left along a grass path between hedges. Cross the River Glem on a long metal bridge. Then go half right on a path through rough ground and cross a ditch on a timber bridge. Leave the Stour Valley Path, which turns right, and keep straight on across a field. Having crossed the field, go roughly straight on beside a tall hedge on the right. In 50 yards turn right over a five-sleeper bridge; then turn left, to continue along a grassy headland with the hedge on the left. At the corner of the field, turn left beside a ditch on the right; continue for a few yards, and then turn right over a culvert and across a field on a path leading towards Parsonage Farm. Pass the farm on the left and continue along a sandy track for a short distance.

5 At the point where the track you are on bends right into a lane, turn left, passing a garage on the right, and cross the shingle drive to the farmhouse. Drop down a little through an area with trees and cross another bridge over the River Glem. Walk along a narrow footpath and then a grass headland path with a hedge on the left. On reaching the road, turn left.

6 In about 100 yards, just before reaching some farm buildings on the right, turn right, as waymarked, along a narrow meandering path. The path swings left over a sleeper bridge and continues along a headland with a hedge on the right. In 100 yards or so, turn right over another sleeper bridge, and then left to continue with the hedge on the left. At a corner where the hedge bends left, keep straight on along a path across a field.

7 At the road turn left, and, in 100 yards, turn right along a narrow footpath between hedges. You soon reach a field, and the path continues beside a hedge on the right. At the corner of the field, observe the waymark and carry straight on, for about 100 yards into the field. There is then a mid-field right turn, along another cross-field path, that should bring you to a tall hedge and an oak tree at a corner of the field. Now follow the hedge on the right, and, at the corner, bend round to the left, still beside the hedge. In a few yards turn right to cross a ditch on a sleeper bridge and continue along a headland with a hedge on the left.

8 At a corner, meet a footpath at right angles and turn left along it, still beside a hedge on the left. Follow the footpath round to the right at the field corner. Soon after, swing left and drop down to the corner of another field.

9 This large field is divided into several paddocks. A series of squeeze stiles defines the route. Make your way generally towards the left-hand end of a building with a clock face in the gable. As you approach the building, turn right immediately after the fifth squeeze stile and negotiate a steel stile. You then come to a sandy exercise area. Skirt left round the fence, and, after crossing the last squeeze stile, go straight on, passing the building and going through a narrow gap in a tall hedge to reach a road.

10 Cross straight over and continue along a headland footpath with a hedge on the left. Eventually come to a cart track and turn left along it, soon to reach the B1064 road opposite the perimeter wall of Melford Hall. Turn left along a minor road roughly parallel to the main road but skirting The Green. Pass Melford Hall gatehouse on the right and continue beside The Green, passing an attractive row of houses on the left, to return to the Black Lion.

Date walk completed:
....

Place of Interest
Melford Hall (National Trust) is a Tudor house set in impressive grounds. There is also a small display relating to Beatrix Potter. Telephone: 01787 880286.

The Swan Inn

From the banks of the River Stour, in the centre of the village, this walk follows lanes and country footpaths to the Ager Fen Nature Reserve, an area of woods and fen in the shallow valley of Assington Brook. At first the return is beside the brook before climbing out of the valley to descend to the River Stour.

Distance: *5½ miles*

OS Explorer 196 Sudbury, Hadleigh and Dedham Vale
GR 904339

A fairly easy walk

Starting point: The car park of the Swan Inn, Bures. If leaving your car, please check with the landlord first. There is a public car park by the village hall in Nayland Road (point 2 on sketch map).

How to get there: From Sudbury, Bures can be reached along the B1508 (about 5 miles). Alternatively, follow the A134 road between Colchester and Sudbury, and, about 4 miles from Sudbury, take a turning to Assington and go from there to Bures.

South of the bridge over the River Stour, on the Essex side of the village, and just a few yards along the road to Lamarsh is the **Swan Inn**. In the two adjacent dining rooms, the ceiling and wall beams, enhanced by gleaming brass ornaments, give a comfortable, old-world charm to the building, said to be at least 300 years old. The menu provides a choice of traditional British fare, together with a selection of Italian dishes and several Indian options, including curry. Greene King Ales are available.

Opening times on Monday to Saturday are noon to 2.30 pm and 6 pm to 9 pm. Sunday (Sunday roast only) noon to 2.30 pm.

Telephone: 01787 228121.

The Walk

1 From the Swan, go right to the road junction and turn right onto the road to Colchester. In about 250 yards, just after the school sign, turn left through a kissing gate along a surfaced footpath. Walk beside the River Stour and cross it on the footbridge to reach the recreation ground. (There is an interesting information board here.) Walk straight on, passing through the public car park, to a road.

2 Turn right and continue along the road, before long turning left at Claypits Lane. Pass Tawneys Ride on the left, and, where the road bends left, keep straight on along a gravel lane. (Just as you come to a wood on the left, pause and look back for a fine view of the Stour Valley.) On reaching the concrete drive to a farm, turn left, still on a lane. Soon pass Cuckoo House on the right before coming to a road.

3 Go right for a short distance; then turn right between white gates to take the concrete farm track passing a number of sheds. Where the concrete ends, go straight on along a well used track beside a hedge on the right. In 100 yards or so, bear round to the left. (Here there is a good view of the country around.)

4 Shortly, where the track turns sharp right to Chapel Barn (an ancient barn that has been restored), go straight on along a wide grassy headland beside a hedge on the right. (Pause, if you will, at the seat overlooking the valley of Assington Brook.) Go down to the corner of the field; climb over a stile under an old hollow oak, and cross the brook on a timber bridge. With a hedge on the left, go straight on through a meadow, crossing a small watercourse to reach the corner of the field.

5 Cross another stile into an enormous field, and go straight up the hill along a well maintained field path. At the top, a gap in the hedge leads into a leafy green lane, which, after passing a cream dwelling on the right, meets a road. Go left, passing an old brick and weather-boarded barn on the left, and, a little

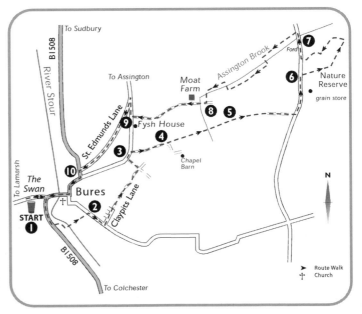

58

further on, a grain store complex on the right.

6 In a short distance, turn right through a kissing gate to enter the Arger Fen Nature Reserve. Keep straight on along the main path, ignoring a couple of minor paths to the left. You eventually come to a field at the edge of the wood, and here the path bears left and immediately re-enters the wood. Now go straight along a grassy path through the forest ride. (Ignore an inviting well-used path to the right.) There is a stand of conifers on the left. Cross a footpath that cuts across obliquely, and keep straight on. Later, your path bends left, skirting a fenced wildlife sanctuary. Descend a little; the fence is on your right. The path swings left again. You are walking roughly along the contour, still beside the fence on the right. The path continues to follow the fence for quite a way, bending left and right, with an occasional boardwalk over soft ground. Eventually, it veers left, climbing away from the fence. Soon climb the few steps that lead to a kissing gate. Leave the reserve, turning right along the road, and walk down the hill to a ford.

7 Cross Assington Brook. (There is a footbridge.) Immediately beyond the stream, turn left through a one-bar gate and walk through a meadow, with the brook on the left. Go through a really substantial gate and continue beside the stream. At the corner of the field, turn left across the brook and continue beside the stream, now on the right. Cross a small ditch by a sleeper bridge and continue as before. A kissing gate and a sleeper bridge lead into the next field. Before long, at a waymark, turn right down some steps, cross a timber bridge over the brook, and

turn left, still beside the stream. Soon there is a small lake on the right. At the far end of the lake swing slightly left on a track which takes you to the opposite side of the brook once again.

8 Before long, reach a right-angled junction and turn right into the lane, with hedges on both sides. Pass the pond and garden of Moat Farm on the right. In about a quarter of a mile, you pass a pair of pink cottages and then come to a road.

9 The walk turns right here. (However, you might make a slight detour of 200 yards to the left to look at Fysh House, a fine Georgian building on the site of an older medieval house.) In 200 yards, at Lark Hill, with a good view to the right, turn left along St Edmund's Lane. Go down the hill into the village.

10 At the T-junction turn left, and, at the junction with Cuckoo Hill, bear right along the road to Colchester. Keep along the village street, and then swing right, passing the church on the left. Cross the River Stour and return to the Swan Inn.

Place of Interest
Sudbury is an ancient market town with a history dating back to Saxon times. It has many beautiful and interesting buildings, including **Gainsborough's House**, the birthplace of Thomas Gainsborough, which now houses an exhibition of his life and work together with the works of other painters. Telephone: 01787 372958.

Date walk completed:
....

The Six Bells

Part of this circular walk is along permissive paths through Bradfield Woods, a national nature reserve,

Distance: *4½ Miles*

OS Explorer 211 Bury St Edmunds & Stowmarket
GR 946570

A walk along grassy forest rides and field paths

Starting point: The Six Bells, Felsham. If leaving the car, please ask the landlord first. Alternative start: Bradfield Woods Nature Reserve, where there is a car park. (Start the walk at point 8.)

How to get there: From the east, leave the A14 Stowmarket to Bury road at the slip road signed to Tostock Beyton and Turston. Turn right into Beyton. Opposite the green, and immediately before the White Horse public house, turn sharp left along a narrow road. Go through Hessett and in 3 miles reach Felsham; bear left to the Six Bells.

managed by the Suffolk Wildlife Trust. There are about 70 hectares of woodland that has been used and cared for since 12th century.

Standing opposite the church in Felsham is the **Six Bells**. Part of this attractive old building is faced with round flints. Freshly cooked food is served in the comfortable bar area and the adjacent restaurant. Whilst providing a good range of traditional English dishes, the menu also offers more unusual fare, for example rabbit Salmorgo, with a sauce of paprika, chilli, olive oil, wine and shallots, and koftas, served in pitta bread envelopes.

Opening times are from noon to 2.30 pm and from 5.30 pm to 11.30 pm, Monday to Friday; from noon to 3.30 pm and 5.30 pm to 11.30 pm on Saturday; and from noon to 3 pm and 5.30 pm to 11.30 pm on Sunday. (No food is served on Tuesday evening.)

Telephone: 01449 736268.

The Walk

1 Cross the road from the Six Bells; walk through the churchyard, passing the church tower on the left, and leave by an old kissing gate in the corner. Continue through the allotments beside a hedge on the right, and, still beside the hedge, to a timber bridge over a stream. Cross the field on a path to a corner and go right, as waymarked, beside a thick hedge on the right.

2 In 20 yards turn right over a sleeper bridge and then left, at first beside the hedge. Continue in the same direction,

passing a pair of mature oaks; go through an uncultivated grassy area, and then beside a ditch on the right. Again turn right to cross a sleeper bridge, and then go left along a headland path beside a hedge on the left. On meeting a cart track, continue beside the hedge to reach a road.

3 Turn left. (In 200 yards pass a byroad to the left; and, just after a bungalow, a footbridge on the right.) Stay on the road for about ¾ mile. A road on the left is signed to Thorpe Morieux; almost opposite this junction, go across a timber footbridge.

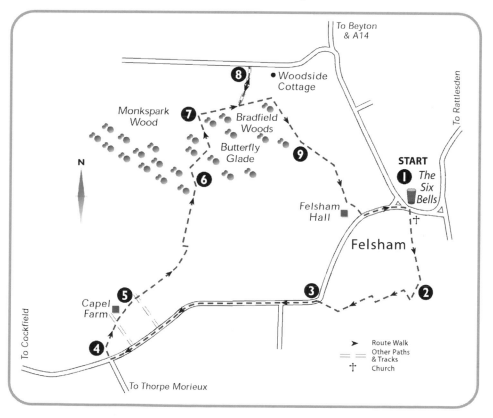

4 Turn diagonally right on a path across a field, heading towards some trees. Cross a stile beside a gate and continue on a narrow path between blackthorn bushes. Soon come out at a grass area and walk on beside a hedge on the right. Turn left at the junction with a farm drive and walk along it for a few yards. Bear right beside an old barn, with a glimpse on the left of beautiful Capel Farm house. After an open yard, cross a stile beside a metal gate and continue along a concrete farm track.

5 Where the track ends, bear slightly left to join a field path. On reaching the field edge continue along a headland, with a narrow wood on the left. At the narrow end of the large field, enter a wood, which you leave in a few yards; turn left and then turn right along a broad headland path beside a tall hedge on the left.

6 At the end of the field, enter Bradfield Wood. Some 10 yards into the wood is a post numbered 18 and bearing a blue arrow. (A few yards away, there is a public bird hide overlooking a small pond surrounded by reeds.) The walk continues straight on. Bend right at a path junction, still following the blue arrow. When you reach the Butterfly Glade (where there is an information board), turn left along the blue route as indicated on post 19. Follow this grassy woodland path almost to the northern edge of Bradfield Wood.

7 Here, by a storage area for forest products, turn right (a sign reads 'to the car park'). Follow the gravel track, passing a stand of recently coppiced hazel. At the next junction of paths, marked by post no.3, take the path to the left leading to the car park and information point. (Here there is a display board about the reserve and leaflets are available. A blackboard gives information about the flora and fauna that can currently be seen.)

8 From the visitors' display area, retrace your steps along the gravel cart track. At the four-way junction, turn left, following the red arrow waymark. Almost at the edge of the wood and within sight of Woodside Cottage, bend right and continue through the wood. On reaching post no.7 at a junction of paths, turn left; soon swing right to follow the edge of the wood. (If you wander a few yards to the left, you can see the medieval bank that surrounds this ancient wood.)

9 At post no. 12, where the path bends right, take a sharp turn to the left, passing a display board, and descend the steps cut into the bank. Cross a plank bridge and continue along a headland path with the hedge on the left. At the field corner, go right and then left and continue along a field edge. At the next corner, bear slightly left along a narrow footpath between fences to join the head of a short cul-de-sac. At the road, turn left to return to the village centre and the start.

Place of Interest
Bradfield Woods National Nature Reserve. It is well worth spending time exploring more of this ancient woodland with its nature trails, bird-watching hide and visitor centre.

Date walk completed:

The Cock

The walk explores part of the Box valley and the area around the village of Polstead, with its many picturesque houses. Here the River Box flows through pleasant rural scenery to join the River Stour and delightful woods complete the scene.

Distance: *4 miles*

OS Explorer 196 Sudbury, Hadleigh & Dedham Vale
GR 994383

A moderate walk

Starting point: The Cock car park (please seek landlord's agreement). There is a lay-by on the green opposite the Cock.

How to get there: Polstead is about 1 mile north of Stoke-by-Nayland. From the A12, take the B1068 to Stoke-by-Nayland. A few yards beyond the village centre, turn right along a minor road. At the pond, turn right up the hill to reach the green and the pub.

The Cock, a 17th-century inn, stands on the north side of the village green. Alongside the traditionally-styled bar are two spacious and airy dining rooms overlooking the green. One of the rooms is decorated with pictures of vintage Second World War aircraft. The fare includes several interesting dishes such as salmon fillet in lemon and butter sauce, served on a bed of mixed vegetables and new potatoes. Suffolk huffers, locally baked soft baps, offered with 28 different options of fillings are very popular. Adnams and Greene King IPA are the ales served, together with an occasional guest ale.

Opening times are Tuesday to Saturday 11 am to 3 pm and 6 pm to 11 pm; Sunday 12 noon to 3 pm and 6 pm to 10.30 pm. Open all day on summer weekends.

Telephone: 01206 263150.

The Walk

1 From the green, walk down the hill on the road to Stoke-by-Nayland. A plaque on a terrace of thatched cottages on the left commemorates Charles Colston, a painter. Pass the pond on the right and at the road junction go straight over through a steel kissing-gate into the Horsecroft, a large meadow. Pass Polstead church on the right and continue, making for the right-hand side of a white bungalow.

2 Leave by a kissing-gate and keep straight on along a road. Cross the River Box, and then, opposite Mill Lane on the right, turn left over a stile and walk through a long meadow keeping beside the field boundary on the right.

3 Eventually, at the entrance to a farmyard, turn right as signed, and then left along a headland path that, after leaving the field edge, comes out to a road. Turn left, and pass Scotland Place on the left.

4 Cross the River Box again and in a few yards turn left over a sleeper bridge and

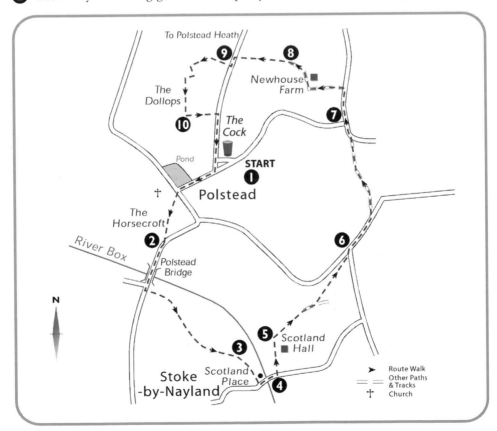

through a kissing-gate into a meadow. Walk straight across to a fence at a corner and continue beside the fence on the right, behind which is Scotland Hall.

5 Look out for and go over a stile in the fence on the right. Immediately after this, cross a timber bridge, and 10 yards beyond, go straight on at the junction of paths. Pass a tall Wellingtonia tree on the right. The well-marked path makes a left and right turn to climb a slight rise beside a mature conifer wood. At the top, leave the cart track half left along a grass path through a new plantation, passing some industrial buildings on the right. Soon enter a pine wood. You may care to rest and take refreshment at the picnic table in the wood. Continue along this very pleasant woodland path and eventually reach a road at a three-way junction.

6 Keep straight on towards Hadleigh. Some 20 yards beyond the imposing gate of Spring Hill, bear left along a narrow leafy lane, which in about a quarter of a mile meets a track with hedges both sides. Turn right along it and soon meet a road at a bend and go straight on.

7 At the road junction, continue straight on, but soon turn left along the concrete drive to Newhouse Farm (Polstead Animal Feeds). Go to the left of the main buildings and follow 'All traffic' signs through the farmyard. On reaching a pond on the left, keep straight on. The farmhouse is behind a brick wall on the right, and soon you will see a cricket ground on the left.

8 Pass a cottage on the right, and keep straight on along a grass track that in about a quarter of a mile reaches a road.

Polstead church

9 Turn left for about 50 yards and then turn right along a grass path between hedges. Cross a stile and immediately turn left along a narrow footpath between a hedge on the right and a rabbit fence on the left. The path turns left at a corner and in about 50 yards bends right and enters woods, called The Dollops. Walk through this delightful deciduous wood, which is carpeted with bluebells in the spring.

10 The path bends left and climbs out of a shallow valley to leave the wood. Continue along the edge of a field and come out to a road. Turn right and you will soon reach Polstead village green and the start.

Place of Interest

Stoke-by-Nayland, just to the south of Polstead, is well worth a visit if only to see the wonderful church of St Mary. It features in several of John Constable's paintings and its fine 15th-century tower can be viewed from miles around.

Date walk completed:

....

Rickinghall

The White Horse

This circular walk from the twin villages of Rickinghall and Botesdale, sets out northwards across wide fields to Redgrave, passing an entrance to Redgrave Fen, a marshy area where the River Waveney rises. The county boundary with Norfolk is just a quarter of a mile away.

The **White Horse** is a pleasant and comfortable village inn. There is a covered patio with tables, overlooking a lawn and children's play area at the rear. Lavish portions are provided from a menu that includes many of our traditional dishes, such as steak and ale pie, cod and chips, and the all-day breakfast. Pasta dishes are also available, as are jacket potatoes with a selection of fillings.

Opening times are from noon to 3 pm and from 5 pm to 11 pm on weekdays; and from noon to 11 pm at the weekend. Food is available from noon to 2 pm and 6.30 pm to 8.30 pm, Tuesday to Sunday.

Telephone: 01379 898303.

Distance: *6 or 5 miles*

OS Explorer 230 Diss and Harleston GR 045756

An easy walk along well-defined tracks and field paths

Starting point: The White Horse, Rickinghall. Alternatively, by starting at the war memorial, the length of the walk could be reduced by about a mile. If leaving your car at the White Horse car park, please check with the landlord first. There are also lay-bys on the village street nearer the war memorial.

How to get there: From the A143 road between Bury St Edmunds and Diss, follow the signs to Botesdale and Rickinghall. The White Horse is on the main street, towards the western end of the village.

The Walk

1 From The White Horse, walk for about half a mile eastwards to the war memorial. Bear left at the memorial and pass pink Old Cock House on the left. In about 100 yards, bear left again, passing Corner Cottage on the right. This road serves a number of attractive old cottages and newer houses that have been carefully designed to fit into the street scene.

2 Where the road makes a right turn, go straight on across a lawn and into a field, as waymarked. Go across the meadow, at one point crossing a concrete bridge over a stream.

3 At the field boundary, cross a footpath and keep straight on along a well-maintained path across a very large field. At its end, join a track, passing a cream dwelling on the right. Where the gravel access track bends right, go straight on along a narrow footpath for a few yards, and then turn half right along a cart track leading to a road. Here turn left to go into Redgrave, passing Half Moon Lane on the right.

4 At the pond, turn right into Church Way, passing the green on the left and pausing perhaps to rest in the shelter or on the seat carved from a massive log. 100 yards beyond the green, turn left along a gravel track that soon becomes a grass path. Later there is a hedge on the left. At the corner of the field, go on, dropping down along a narrow footpath beside a wood on the right. Pass a pink cottage on the right and continue along the drive to a road. (Straight ahead here is the entrance to Redgrave Fenn Nature Reserve, the source of the River Waveney.)

5 Turn left along the road, and on reaching a crossroads, go straight on along Hinderclay Road. Pass the entrance to a factory on the right and soon after, where the road bends right, go left along a wide gravel track, passing a small water treatment plant on the left. The path now continues as a

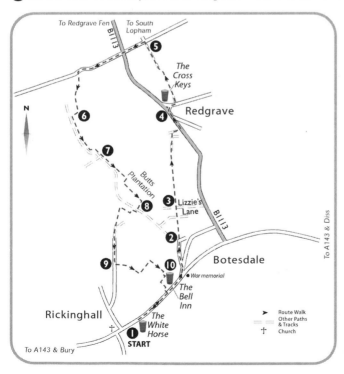

67

grassy lane with ditches on both sides.

6 At the end of the lane, enter a field and turn right beside a ditch. At the corner of the field, turn left to follow a stream on the right. Make a dog-leg left and right, still along the river bank. (This stream flows into the head waters of the Little Ouse river that joins the River Great Ouse, ultimately flowing into the Wash.)

Redgrave village green

7 After crossing a track leading to a bridge on the right, the path, still beside the river, is more like a cart track. Soon go right and left over a ditch and continue with the ditch on the left; later there is a narrow wood on the left.

8 Look out for a three-way footpath sign and turn right on a narrow but well used path across the meadow. Cross a concrete bridge and turn right, as signed, beside the river. In 50 yards, turn left through a small wood, and then right over a wooden bridge. Continue between a hedge on the right and a fence on the left. Cross another footbridge and go through a kissing gate to turn left along a headland path. Go through a gap into the next field and go out through another kissing gate onto a grass lane. Bearing right, join a farm road and continue along it for nearly a quarter of a mile. Pass a signed footpath to the right and one to the left.

9 Soon after passing a bungalow on the left, turn left on a well used footpath between hedges. Later it is a wide headland path with a hedge on the left. Turn left, still beside the hedge on the left. Turn right at a three-way footpath sign

and continue along a broad track with a shelter belt of trees on the left.

10 Cross a bridge over a deep stream, and turn right along a narrow footpath. The path bends left, following a ditch on the right. Next, the path takes a right turn, now with a wide ditch on the left. A left turn over a timber bridge brings you to a narrow path that zigzags between houses to reach the road in Rickinghall. Turn right, and walk back to the White Horse (½ mile).

Place of Interest

Redgrave and Lopham Fen, accessible from point 5 on the walk, is a 360-acre nature reserve, in the care of Suffolk Wildlife Trust. It comprises reed and sedge beds, reeds still being harvested here for thatching. The sources of the rivers Waveney (flowing eastwards towards Lowestoft) and the Little Ouse (flowing westwards to the great Ouse) can be found here, just a few yards apart.

Date walk completed:

....

The Red Lion

This walk is through part of the Dedham Vale. It passes the tiny settlement of Flatford, with its mill, Bridge Cottage and Willie Lott's house, places that have been immortalized in the landscape paintings of John Constable, who lived at East Bergholt.

Distance: *5 miles*

OS Explorer 196 Sudbury, Hadleigh and Dedham Vale
GR 069347

An easy walk along well-defined tracks and field paths

Starting point: The public car park adjacent to the Red Lion, East Bergholt.

How to get there: From the A12 (Colchester to Ipswich), take the B1070 towards East Bergholt. In half a mile turn right along Hadleigh Road, and turn left at the next junction. A further right turn brings you to the car park, the Red Lion, and the village centre.

In the centre of East Bergholt, not far from the church, stands the **Red Lion**. Meals are served in the lounge bar, in an adjoining dining room, and also in the garden. As well as a fine range of traditional meals, this popular pub offers a good selection of vegetarian dishes: chestnut casserole; leek, cheese and horseradish bake; and red lentil and spinach curry among them.

Opening times are from 11.30 am to 3 pm and 6 pm to 11 pm on weekdays, and from noon to 4 pm and 6 pm to 10.30 pm on Sundays.

Telephone: 01206 298332.

69

The Walk

1 From the village car park, walk to the road and turn right, passing the Red Lion on the right. In a few yards, turn right along a side road, passing the post office at the corner. Past the Congregational church, at the entrance gate to Vale Farm, take the small gate immediately left of the farm gate and drop down into a shallow valley on a narrow footpath between fences. Cross a wooden footbridge and a gravel drive; continue straight on between fences, climbing out of the valley. At the top of the hill a gate leads into a wider path, still between fences.

2 Turn left by a four-way sign at the end of the field and continue along Dead Lane, a narrow sunken lane between hedges. At the end of the lane, turn left at a T-junction; now you are walking beside a hedge on the right and a fence on the left. Continue straight on. Later the path runs through a narrow band of woodland. On reaching a T-junction with a wide grassy path, turn right along it for about 50 yards.

3 Turn left across a stile, cross a sleeper bridge, and turn right. Do not cross the tempting stile but turn left on a narrow path through a small wood. Soon cross another stile into a field and continue beside the hedge on the right. Bear right across a stile and continue, now with a hedge on the left. Cross a stile and follow a hedge on the right and a fence on the left. Another stile brings you into a meadow. Follow the boundary on the left and exit by a stile.

4 Turn right along Fen Lane, a cart track between hedges. Cross a backwater of the River Stour on a wide timber bridge, and continue to the end of the lane; here cross Fen Bridge, a substantial timber footbridge over the Stour.

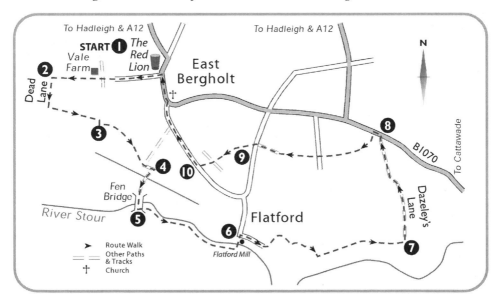

5 Turn left and walk beside the river on your left, eventually reaching Flatford Bridge, which you cross. *(If you wish to see the lock and Flatford Mill from the riverside, before recrossing the river, continue straight on for about 200 yards downstream. Then return to the bridge.)*

6 Pass Bridge Cottage on the right and turn right along a road. (The National Trust café and visitors' centre is on the right.) Continue along the narrow road, passing Flatford Mill, now a field centre, and then cream-painted Willy Lott's cottage. Swing left at the field centre car park, and keep left to continue along a grass path beside a wood on the left and a tall hedge on the right. Bend right at a corner, still along the grass path, which soon bends left. Look out for a Stour Valley Path waymark, and turn left onto a much narrower path. Bend right and cross a stile into a meadow. Keep beside a hedge on the right as it bends to the right, passing an electricity pylon. Cross a stile in the corner and turn left beside the hedge on the left. The path continues for about half a mile, following the hedge on the left, and crossing four stiles en route.

7 Look out for a metal gate on the left, giving access to a broad lane between hedges. Cross a stile beside the gate and walk up Dazeley's Lane to come to a road (the B1070); turn left for a few yards.

8 Immediately after 1 Clarence Villas, turn left, as signed, along a very narrow path beside a garden fence on the right. Go across the field that you come to. At the far side, after passing through an uncultivated area, continue with a hedge on the left. Leave by a wooden farm gate and cross straight over a cul-de-sac. Then

follow the headland path with a hedge on the left. A stile takes you into the next field, where you keep straight on. At the corner of the field, come out to an access track and pass a white shed on the right; 50 yards before the road junction, the right of way turns half right across the corner of a pasture, but, as there are no stiles, walk down to the road and turn right.

9 In about 10 yards, leave the road and follow a narrow footpath on the left between a fence and a tall hedge. Descend a little and cross a brook on a concrete bridge. Continue through the ash grove and along the grassy path out of the valley. Cross the farm track (stiles both sides), and walk straight across a pasture to a stile onto a road.

10 Take the footpath behind the roadside hedge. With the road on the left, follow the footpath to its end; then continue along the road to reach a junction with East Bergholt church opposite. Turn left. Passing the site of John Constable's childhood home, return to the Red Lion and the start.

Place of Interest

Bridge Cottage (National Trust), situated just upstream from Flatford Mill, houses an exhibition featuring the work and times of John Constable. There is a tea garden, shop and information centre. Telephone: 01206 298260.

Date walk completed:

....

71

The Black Horse Inn

Thorndon is in the north of Suffolk, roughly midway between Debenham and Eye. The Mid-Suffolk Path, a regional long distance route from Stowmarket to the Angles Way near Hoxne, runs through the village, and about half of this circular walk follows its route.

Distance: 6½ miles

OS Explorer 230 Diss and Harleston GR 137698

A longer walk along lanes and woodland paths

Starting point: The Black Horse Inn, Thorndon. If leaving your car, please check with the landlord first. Otherwise park in the village.

How to get there: Use the A140 road between Ipswich and Norwich. At the White Horse Inn crossroads at Stoke Ash, turn eastwards to Thorndon, 2 miles away.

Standing well back from the street, the **Black Horse Inn** is located by its sign, a three dimensional rampant black horse. Considerably modernized, the building still retains some of the original 16th-century beams. In cool weather a fire burns in the massive brick fireplace. The menu, that changes daily, comprises four or five freshly cooked main course dishes, such as battered cod and chips, Thai curry, or cheese platter. Baguettes, with a choice of five different fillings, are served with salad and crisps. Adman's and Greene King Ales are available, as is the local Aspal Cider.

Opening times are from noon to 2.30 pm; evening opening time is from 6 pm (5 pm on Friday) to 11 pm, and from 7 pm to 10.30 pm on Sundays. Food is served between noon and 2 pm and 7 pm and 9 pm.

Telephone: 01379 678523.

The Walk

1 From the Black Horse, go down Fen View, the road opposite. At the end of the cul-de-sac, take the narrow, almost sunken, footpath with a hedge on the left. Cross a timber footbridge and continue along the path, first through uncultivated land and then through mixed woodland. On leaving the wood, turn right into a field. In about 20 yards, go right through the hedge, cross a sleeper bridge and stile, and immediately turn left. Walk through the field (there is a stream on the right.) Make your way to a stile near the corner diagonally opposite to go out onto a road.

2 Turn right along the road and continue for about a quarter of a mile. At the first hedge on the left, turn left along a headland path beside the hedge on the left. At the corner of the field, go on for a few yards along a broad grass way, and then go half-right to a timber bridge over the River Dove. A metal gate leads into a meadow, which you cross to a stile beside another metal gate, to continue along a narrow sunken lane.

3 At the end of the lane join a cart track, as signed. Go past the ruins of St Mary's church, and then past Old Church Farm. Leave the farm precinct to join a surfaced road. In 10 yards, opposite a small cottage, go right at a bridleway sign onto a narrow leafy lane, with extensive orchards on the left. After nearly half a mile, the lane opens out to a wider farm track between hedges.

4 At the road, go left for a few yards. Turn right along a wide grassy lane with hedges on both sides: a waymark indicates that you have joined the Heart of Suffolk Horse Route. Later, there is a hedge on the left and further on, a ditch on the right. After passing through a small wood, mostly on the right, the grass track runs just inside a wood, Steggall's Wood, that extends to the left, passing a farm on the right.

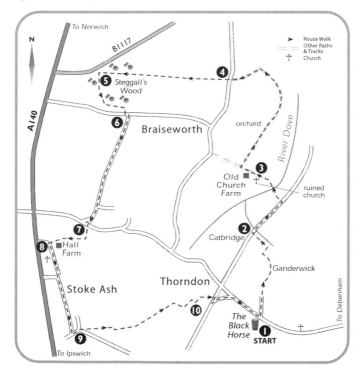

73

5 About 50 yards beyond the last building, leave the lane, turning left along a narrow clearing through the wood. On leaving the wood, cross a shallow ditch, into a field with a wooden electricity pole in mid field. Keeping well to the right of the pole, make your way along the path to a corner of a wood. Here, turn left, roughly following the overhead wires, to meet a hedge. Keep beside the hedge on the right until you find a track on the right that leads out to a road.

6 Go left for 50 yards, and then turn right at the road junction. Follow this quiet road for about half a mile, passing Quiet Acres, an isolated pargetted pink cottage on your way. Keep right at the three-way junction.

7 At the next junction, by a grass triangle, go straight over onto a path across a field. On the far side of the field, go through a gap in the hedge and turn right. Walk beside a hedge on the right, cross a bridge over a deep stream, and pass a white farmhouse away to the left. Keeping beside a ditch on the right, go to a road.

8 Turn left and pass Stoke Ash church. At the junction with the access road to Hill Farm, go right, and, almost immediately, turn left through Stoke Ash village. Soon after passing the post office on the left, turn left into Deadmans Lane.

9 A few yards after a sharp right turn, leave the road to go left onto a grassy headland path, part of the Mid-Suffolk Footpath. At the next field, turn right and left to follow the headland (boundary on the right). At the corner of the field, cross

a four-sleeper bridge and keep straight on across the field towards the left-hand corner of a mature poplar plantation. Continue along the headland beside the plantation on the right. Near its end, go diagonally right through the plantation, as signed, and continue through a wood with a hedge on the left.

10 Turn right and cross a substantial timber bridge. Immediately go left through uncultivated land, following the stream on the left, and then enter a narrow belt of woodland. Cross a sleeper bridge and continue along a pleasant grassy path through a young plantation. Cross another sleeper bridge and keep straight on to come out at a road; go right for just a few yards, and then turn left along the road signed to Debenham. Bear right at the next junction to return to the Black Horse.

Places of Interest

Eye, 3 miles away, is a small market town with a well-marked town trail. There are also the ruins of a motte and bailey castle and the remains of the Priory of St Peter, a Benedictine monastery founded in 1080.

Mid-Suffolk Light Railway Museum, Brockford, near Stowmarket (3 miles), is set in peaceful Suffolk countryside and aims to recreate the tranquility of rail travel between the 1930s and 1950s. Telephone: 01449 766899.

Date walk completed:

....

The Admiral's Head

The tiny River Fynn flows from Witnesham, through a shallow valley, to Martlesham Creek and thence into the Deben Estuary. This walk through part of the Fynn Valley links the villages of Playford and Little Bealings.

Distance: *5 Miles*

OS Explorer 197 Ipswich, Felixstowe and Harwich
GR 230479

An easy walk along well-marked footpaths

Starting point: The car park at the Admiral's Head, Little Bealings (please seek the landlord's permission). There is also a public car park at Playford village hall at point 3 (see sketch map).

How to get there: Follow the A12 to the Martlesham roundabout and then take the A1214 towards Ipswich. Go straight on at the traffic signals, and, very soon after, turn right along Hall Road (signed to Little Bealings). Go straight on at the crossroads to reach the Admiral's Head in the middle of the village (½ mile).

The Admiral's Head is an old pub that has had extensive refurbishment and modernization over the years. The three dining areas are light and spacious. Each area is on a different level and this adds to the charm of the place, giving a feeling of some intimacy. The lunchtime menu provides interesting and unusual fare. The seafood chowder is delicious. Omelette with a choice of smoked salmon and cheese or bacon and mushroom is on offer. There is a fuller evening menu.

Opening times are from noon to 2 pm and from 6.30 pm to 9 pm, Tuesday to Saturday; and from noon to 3 pm on Sunday.

Telephone: 01473 625912.

The Walk

1 From the Admiral's Head, walk along Sandy Lane, a narrow surfaced road, passing the primary school on the right, and at the road junction keep left. Where the road bends right, ignore a sandy area to the left and keep straight on, as signed, along a narrow footpath between bushes. The path descends through woodland and marshy ground to cross a culvert over a small brook. Climb out of the valley.

2 At the top, go through a kissing gate into a pasture. Go straight on beside a fence – and, later, a tall hedge – on the right. At a kissing gate under an old oak, go through the hedge. Turn left along a headland path, with the hedge on the left. The path leads out past a brick cottage on the left. Drop down to a road and go along it. Turn left at the road junction along Hill Farm Road and walk into Playford.

3 Come to a junction where there is a grass triangle and turn right, and in about 50 yards swing left along Brook Lane. The road ends opposite a pair of cottages. Turn left for about 20 yards, and then go right, through a kissing gate, into a meadow and continue beside a fence on the right. At the far end of this long field, leave through another kissing gate and follow a narrow footpath through mixed woodland and later through marshy ground. Cross a sleeper bridge and continue on past a mature willow plantation. On leaving the trees, continue beside a fence on the left.

4 At the T-junction with a well-used gravel track, turn left along it. Cross a bridge over the River Fynn, and soon, where the track bends right, turn left along a grassy, uphill path. On the right is the railway line. Continue roughly parallel to the railway across the open hill; then, by a wooden electricity pole, enter a wood. Walk along this narrow somewhat winding path through the wood and eventually cross a timber

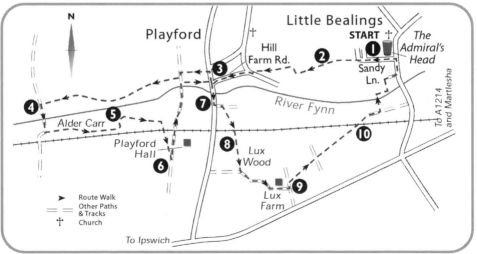

76

bridge by an overflow weir that drains a pond on the right. The narrow footpath gradually bends left and descends into the valley. At the bottom cross two narrow sleeper bridges and leave the wood at a kissing gate to enter a meadow.

5 Turn right beside a hedge on the right. You will probably realize that you previously walked along the other side of this long meadow. A few yards from the field corner, turn right across a two-step stile, and, after crossing a timber bridge over a shallow watercourse, continue straight on through a pasture.

6 At the far corner, go through a farm gate and make a U-turn to the left to walk back along a grassy way between fences, passing Playford Hall away to the right. Cross the River Fynn; in ten yards, turn right over a wooden footbridge and continue beside a young plantation. At the road (with Hill Farm Road, where you were earlier, opposite), turn right.

7 In a few yards, cross the river again, and, in 200 yards, just before the drive to Playford Hall on the right, turn left along a gravel track. At the waymark, turn right, passing an electricity pole, and cross a meadow towards a stile in the opposite fence. Cross the railway, negotiating stiles on both sides, and continue along a field path towards the right-hand edge of Lux Wood.

8 Enter a grassy lane with a hedge on the right and the wood on the left. The lane comes out at the corner of the wood to a hard cart-track. Turn left, towards the farm. At the farm, turn left, as signed, and walk between silos and other farm buildings.

9 Pass Lux Farm house on the left; keep straight on, at first beside a hedge on the left, and soon across a field. Go through a field boundary marked by a row of mature trees, and, after crossing a cart track, continue in the same direction on a cross-field path. On the far side of the field, go through into another field and continue, still straight on, towards a gate in the railway fence.

10 Go through the kissing gate and cross the railway. On the far side, after a two-step stile, bend right through an area of bracken, and walk towards the left-hand corner of some farm buildings. Cross a sleeper bridge over a narrow stream and swing right along a track towards the building. Just before the farm, turn left along a narrow path passing the side of the building on the right. After a few bends, the footpath leads to a substantial footbridge over the Fynn. Turn right and follow the river on the right. Later, bend left and then right to join a track that leads out to a road. Turn left here, and walk back to the Admiral's Head and the start.

Place of Interest
Sutton Hoo (National Trust), the site of an Anglo-Saxon ship burial. An exhibition hall houses a full-size reconstruction of the burial chamber discovered in 1939. Telephone 01394 389700.

Date walk completed:

....

The Swan

Fressingfield is an attractive village deep in rural Suffolk. This walk uses a number of permissive paths that have been opened up in the vicinity of the village.

Distance: *5½ miles*

OS Explorer 230 Diss and Harleston GR 260775

A mixture of quiet roads, field paths and lanes

Starting point: The Swan. If leaving your car there, please check with the landlord. There is also a village car park in Gull Street. (Turn off the B1116 at the war memorial, signed to Cratfield, and turn right just after the Baptist church.)

How to get there: Fressingfield is on the B1116 road between Framlingham and Harleston, about 5 miles south of Harleston.

Near the church, on the main road through the village, stands **the Swan**. It has a spacious bar area and several interconnected dining rooms, decorated in a traditional style. The menu includes a good selection of main dishes such as fresh Lowestoft cod in a broadside beer batter; freshly made lasagne; and steamed steak and kidney suet pudding. There are also several salad options, and freshly baked baguettes with a choice of five different fillings. Adnams Ales and local Aspal cider are served.

Opening times are from 11.30 am to 2.30 pm and from 6 pm to 11 pm. Meals are served from noon to 2 pm and from 6.30 pm to 9 pm.

Telephone: 01379 586280.

The Walk

1 From the Swan, walk down to the war memorial and turn right along the road signed to Cratfield. Just after the Baptist church, turn right along an access road leading to Gull Street. Pass the village car park, and, at the end of the cul-de-sac, continue along a footpath to the B1116.

2 Turn left and continue along the road for about 300 yards. Soon after a house called 'Oaklands', on the left, go left, as signed, through a metal gate along a wide grassy path with a hedge on the left. Towards the end of the field, bear left through the hedge, and then slightly right, to continue through an uncultivated field, walking in the same direction as before. On reaching a corner, turn right.

3 Soon cross a culvert with handrails, and bear right along a signed permissive path, soon to follow a timber walkway beside a stream on the right. Thereafter, the path continues parallel to the stream but further from it. (A plantation of young trees on the left was planted as an amenity, with the help of the Forestry Commission.) Cross a timber bridge and cross a cart track leading to Tithe Farm. Keep straight on, the permissive path continuing as before. Turn right over a four-sleeper bridge, as waymarked, and continue beside a hedge.

4 Turn right, crossing a ditch on another sleeper bridge, to join a public footpath which goes left along a headland, with a ditch on the left. Eventually, you come to a corner where the hedge on the left bends left. Here there is a plank bridge on the left, marked by a footpath sign. (In fact there are four footpaths meeting within a

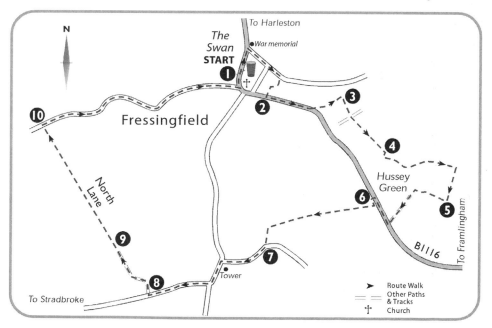

few yards of this point.) Go almost straight ahead on a cross-field path towards a small clump of trees, to reach a farm track beside a pond. Turn right along the track. Just beyond the pond, at a three-way footpath sign close to the hedge on the left, keep straight on, roughly beside the hedge. At a field boundary, cross the ditch and continue straight on beside a hedge on the left.

5 Where the hedge ends at a pond, turn right across the field towards a clump of vegetation surrounding another pond. The path swings half-left towards a wood, which you enter along a narrow footpath to reach the end of what may have once been a wide green lane. Walk down between the hedges to come out to an open field; keep straight on along a cart track beside a hedge on the left. Turn right along the road and continue for about 250 yards.

6 Turn left through a wide gap in the hedge, and, in 10 yards, turn left to follow a permissive path at the edge of a field. At the field corner, bend right and follow the grass path, with a ditch on the left. After passing a small pond, you will have a ditch on the right. Later, follow a hedge on the left; the ditch is now further away on the right. At the small wood, keep straight on between the wood and a hedge on left. At the corner, cross a sleeper bridge to reach a cart track. Go straight on along a permissive path across a field. At the oak tree on the far, side turn left beside a ditch on the right for about 15 yards. Turn right over a sleeper bridge, and then turn left along a headland path with a hedge on the left. At the field corner go right for about 20 yards, and then turn left over a plank bridge out to a road.

7 Turn right onto the road and continue past Oxbridge Farm on the left to a T-junction. Turn left along the road towards Stradbroke, passing a water tower on the left. Follow the road as it bends round to the right, passing the junction on the left to Wilby and Worlingworth. Continue along the road for about ¼ mile.

8 Turn right along a gravel track between hedges. The lane bends left a little as you pass a dwelling on the right. Note a narrow timber footbridge off to the right, and soon after, pass a house on the left.

9 The lane seems to end at a narrow wood. Go straight on along a narrow path and you will find that you are in a lane, known as North Lane, with tall hedges on both sides. At the field, continue in the same direction beside the hedge on the left. Halfway along, at a sign, swing left through the hedge to return to the lane with hedges on both sides. Continue along North Lane until you come to a road.

10 Turn right along the road and walk back to Fressingfield. At the road junction in the village, turn left along the B1116, back to the start.

Place of Interest
Laxfield and District Museum, 5 miles from Fressingfield, has among its various collections, a display of rural, domestic and working life. Telephone: 01986 798421.

Date walk completed:

The Castle Inn

Afterpassing through the castle grounds, the walk skirts The Mere, now a nature reserve,

Distance: *3 miles*

OS Explorer 212 Woodbridge and Saxmundham
GR 286635

A short, easy walk

Starting point: The car park adjacent to the Castle Inn. There are other car parks in the town (look out for the signs).

How to get there: Framlingham is just off the A1120 (Stowmarket to Yoxford) road; or, from the south, use the A12 (London to Lowestoft) road and at the interchange near Wickham Market take the B1116 to Framlingham. Follow the one-way system through the town centre, looking out for the tourist signs to The Castle.

passes the playingfield of Framlingham College and circles the farmland to the north-east of the town. The return provides views of the castle and the town.

Standing almost at the entrance to Framlingham Castle, the **Castle Inn** is a busy and popular establishment. There is a courtyard at the rear with outdoor tables, as well as several tables outside at the front. The menu provides a good choice of fare with such dishes as chicken, leek and bacon in a cream sauce; Suffolk ham, eggs and chunky chips, with a salad garnish; and locally caught cod. There are also several different pasta dishes on offer.

Opening times are from noon to 5 pm each day. Closed Wednesdays.

Telephone: 07903 991748.

The Walk

1 From the Castle Inn go along the drive towards the castle entrance. Immediately before the brick parapet of a bridge over the moat, turn left through an unusual turnstile. As you descend, you will see The Mere and beyond it Framlingham College, an independent school. Cross a bridge over a valley and turn left, climbing up to the castle ramparts. Walk along the top of a grass bank that drops away on the left. Go down the few steps to a bridge and stile to leave the castle precincts. Go straight on along a broad path between bushes; then go through a kissing gate and continue along the path. Cross a concrete footbridge to reach the Framlingham College sports ground.

2 Turn right and skirt the playing field; at the corner, bear round to the left, still along the boundary, with a ditch on the right. At the far corner, cross a timber footbridge and continue through some trees onto a road; turn left. Before long, the road bends slightly left and you pass the entrance to Little Lodge on the right.

3 In a further 50 yards or so, go through a kissing gate on the right, and follow the hedge on the left for about 50 yards. Turn right, climbing slightly beside a well trimmed hedge on the right, with a golf playing area on the left.

4 At the top of the rise turn right, going downhill between a hedge on the left and a fence on the right. Cross a timber bridge, go through a gate, and turn left along a wide strip between fences. Cross a two-step stile into a meadow and immediately turn right beside a fence for 20 yards. Then turn left to walk straight across the meadow.

5 On the far side of the field, cross a stile beside a stream on the right, and then in about 20 yards turn right over a timber bridge. Walk straight on up a slight bank, and continue beside a hedge – and, later, a ditch – on the right. At the field corner,

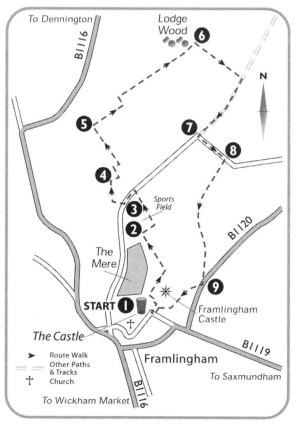

To Dennington
Lodge Wood
B1116
N
5
6
7
8
4
Sports Field
3
2
B1120
The Mere
START **1**
9
Framlingham Castle
The Castle
➤ Route Walk
– – Other Paths & Tracks
† Church
Framlingham
B1119
To Saxmundham
To Wickham Market
B1116

turn left, following a ditch on the right. Go right at a double electricity pole along a grass path underneath the wires and beside a ditch on the right. Later veer slightly left on the grass path to skirt the edge of Lodge Wood on the left.

❻ At the far corner of the wood turn right beside a hedge and ditch on

Inside the castle walls

the right. Pass the end of a young conifer plantation on the left and keep straight on, still beside the hedge. Meet a surfaced farm drive by a concrete hard standing and turn right.

❼ The drive, with hedges both sides, ends at a pair of wooden farm gates. Here you join the public road at a corner, and turn left.

❽ In a little under 200 yards, at the top of the slight rise, turn right, as signed, and follow a grassy field edge path with a hedge on the left. Soon, straight ahead, there is a clear view of Framlingham Castle. Keep along the headland path, which swings left a little and descends into a shallow valley. Cross a wooden bridge in the valley bottom and continue up the other side to the diagonally opposite corner of the field. Here go out to the road.

❾ In a few yards, turn right into a grassy meadow and bear round to the left. After

passing through a small wood, swing right and come to the corner of recreation ground. With the massive castle walls to the right, walk down, and, skirting the castle moat, go out to the castle approach road. Turn left to go back to the start.

Place of Interest

Framlingham Castle (English Heritage), built in the late 12th century for Roger Bigod, Earl of Norfolk, a man of great influence at the court of Henry II, is an imposing sight with its massive walls, crenellated towers and tall Tudor chimneys. In the 16th century the castle served as a prison, and later in its history a poorhouse and school were built in the grounds. In addition to the castle, its outer courts, moats and grounds, there is an exhibition and shop to be visited. Telephone: 01728 724189

Date walk completed:

....

83

The Fleece

Bungay is a small market town in the north of Suffolk. The River Waveney makes a wide, almost circular loop on the edge of the town. The meadows within the loop form Outney Common. The walk starts in the town centre, and, after passing the ruins

Distance: *5½ miles*

OS Outdoor Leisure 40 The Broads
GR 336896

An easy walk across water meadows and along lanes

Starting point: Priory Lane pay-and-display car park.

How to get there: Follow the A143 Bury to Great Yarmouth road. At a roundabout, take the A144 through the town towards Halesworth. Pass Market Place, and, just after the church on the left, turn right into narrow Priory Lane to get to the car park.

of Bigod's Castle, crosses Outney Common and swings round through woods, on higher ground overlooking the river.

The Fleece stands in the centre of Bungay, opposite the priory church of St Mary. Around the bar area are several separate rooms including a non-smoking dining room and a snug. Among the dishes on the menu are seafood platter; grilled rump steak with onion rings, mushrooms, tomatoes, fries, peas and a side salad; and home-made lasagne. For a lighter meal, jacket potatoes are served with five options for fillings. There is also a children's menu. Adnams ales are available.

Opening times are from 11 am to 11 pm, Monday to Saturday; and noon to 10.30 pm on Sunday. Food is served from noon to 2 pm.

Telephone: 01986 892192.

The Walk

1 From the car park, walk back to the main street and turn left, passing the Fleece on the left and St Mary's church opposite. In a few yards, where the road bends right, turn left under a metal arch bearing the inscription 'Bigod's Castle 12th C'. Bear right by the visitors' centre and follow a surfaced footpath, passing the castle on the right. At the road, turn left along Earsham Street, and, in about 100 yards, turn right into Outney Road. At the end of the cul-de-sac, continue along a footpath leading to a footbridge over the main road.

2 From the bridge, turn right and walk through the golf club car park. At the far end, pick up a Bigod Way sign and walk along a grass path parallel to the golf club access road. Eventually swing left a little to meet a gravel track, that comes from a roundabout on the A143.

3 In less than 100 yards, go right, as waymarked, along a narrower path. After another kissing gate, you will be following a well walked footpath through the meadow. Halfway across, a narrow wooden footbridge takes you over Old River, a part of the River Waveney; then go through another gate. (From this point, the footpath is less clear on the ground.) Make for a metal kissing gate under the trees on the far side of the common.

4 Cross the main arm of the Waveney on a substantial footbridge. (A plaque on the deck reads 'H N Rumsby 1922 Town

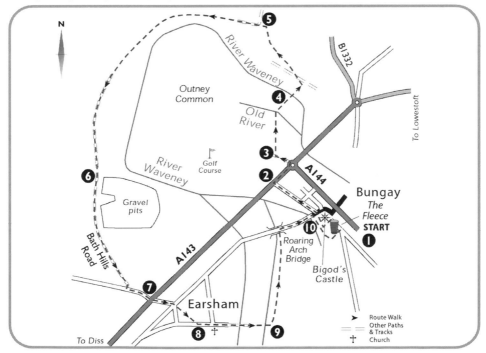

85

Reeve'.) A few yards further on, there is another bridge. The footpath continues through a narrow belt of woodland. Just as you leave the wood, turn left, waymarked 'Bigod Way'. Pass through a gate into a meadow and keep straight on. Soon cross a surfaced drive, and keep straight on up a grassy path climbing the side of the valley. Near the top, cross a stile and continue along a narrow footpath at the edge of the valley, with woodland dropping steeply down on the left, to the valley floor.

5 Swing left and join a road, which soon becomes a narrow lane between hedges. Pass a cottage on the right and another on the left. The lane continues, but now grassy and unsurfaced. Go through a gate, and, soon after passing a dwelling on the left, come to the drive and walk straight on along it. Pass Valley Farm (painted white) on the left to reach a surfaced road, and continue.

6 Passing the entrance to the gravel workings on the left, continue along the road, where you may encounter an occasional gravel lorry. (About 300 yards further on, there is a good view on the left of the extensive lakes developed from former gravel pits.) Go past a row of cottages built in 1927 on the right, and keep straight on. At the road junction bear left along Hall Road.

7 In 200 yards, cross straight over the A143 and take the footpath immediately opposite, which leads into the head of a cul-de-sac. Keep straight on into Earsham village. At the road junction by the war memorial, turn left for about 10 yards, and then go right, to follow a narrow lane, passing the village hall on your right.

Keep in the same direction along a footpath that, after skirting some rear gardens, comes to a road. Turn left along it, waymarked 'Angles Way'.

8 Pass All Saints' church on the right, and at the end of the road, go straight on along a gravel track. Just after some cottages on the right, cross an arm of the River Waveney and continue along the path, with hedges on both sides.

9 Cross a bridge over another arm of the river, and immediately turn left along the riverbank. Cross a stile and continue through a meadow, still with the river on the left. Towards the end of the meadow, pass several mature willow trees, and continue beside the river, eventually to reach a road. Turn right; in just over 200 yards, enter Bungay, crossing the third arm of the river, probably originally its main course.

10 Turn right along Castle Lane. Where it branches, fork left up the hill. Soon leave the lane, turning right along a narrow path that leads to a flight of steps up what was probably the castle ramparts. Then drop down to a grassy play area with picnic tables. Leave through a metal gate to return to the start nearby.

Place of Interest
The Otter Trust at Earsham is one of three such centres in the U.K. offering the opportunity to see otters in semi-natural conditions. Additionally, the three lakes are home to a wide selection of waterfowl. Telephone: 01986 893470.

Date walk completed:
....

river; and Wantisden, a tiny community comprising a few isolated dwellings. Because of the light sandy soil, many of the fields are interspersed with woods, forest, and shelter belts of trees, providing an interesting and varied walk.

Standing at a fork in the road is the **Oyster Inn**. This comfortable and friendly inn is said to be many hundreds of years old, built when oysters were plentiful (there are still oyster beds in the Butley river). In cold weather, there is a warming fire in the dining room, and the rooms are decorated with paintings by a local artist. The regular menu includes favourites such as seafood platter, chips and salad; eggs, bacon, sausages, tomatoes and mushrooms. Look out for the seasonal treats, such as pot-roast partridge and roast pheasant. Vegetarian dishes are also available.

Opening times are from 12 noon to 2 pm and from 6.30 pm to 9 pm, Tuesday to Sunday, but there are seasonal variations.

Telephone: 01394 450790.

This walk links three parishes: Butley; Chillesford, at the head of the tidal estuary of the Butley

Distance: *5½ miles or 6¼ miles*

OS Explorer 212 Woodbridge & Saxmundham
GR 368510

A longer walk along farm tracks and field paths

Starting point: The car park at the Oyster Inn, Butley. If leaving the car, please check with the landlord and park in the overflow car park at the top of the ramp behind the inn.

How to get there: Butley is 4 miles from Orford, on the B1084. From the Melton roundabout on the A12, follow the A1152, signed to Snape. At the fork where the A1152 turns left, keep straight on along the B1084 and follow the bending road for about 4 miles. The Oyster Inn is on the right.

The Walk

1 From the Oyster Inn, turn left; then, almost immediately, turn right along Mill Lane, passing the village hall on the left.

2 On reaching Butley Barns on the left, you can continue along Mill Lane, missing out the loop to Butley church, to shorten the walk by about ¾ mile. However, for the full walk, opposite the barn turn right up a cart track. Soon the track runs beside a hedge on the right. The path bends left and right, still following the hedge. At the corner of the field turn right for a few yards to reach a road. Turn left along the road.

3 Just before reaching St John the Baptist church, Butley, turn left along a gravel lane with hedges both sides. Soon the lane becomes a soft sandy cart-track. Swing left and join a similar track coming in from the right. Keep straight on, pass Low Farm about 100 yards away on the right. In a further half mile rejoin Mill Lane at a grass triangle here.

4 Bear right onto the road. Pass the old watermill on the left and continue into

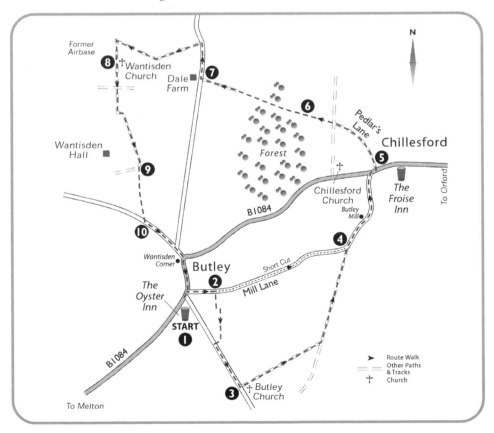

88

Chillesford, about ¼ mile. At the main road turn right for a few yards. (200 yards further along the road is the Froise Inn.)

5 Turn left along Pedlar's Lane, an unsurfaced gravel road. After passing several dwellings on the left, the track becomes a grassy rural lane between hedges. Continue along the lane to reach a junction with a gravelly track in just over quarter of a mile. Keep straight on here, immediately passing a concrete farm storage area on the left, and continue beside a hedge on the left.

6 Reach the corner of a wood on the left. Here the track swings slightly left and right, and you continue along the edge of the wood on the left before coming to a grassy forest ride with woods both sides. At the end of the forest ride, the track you have been following bends left beside the wood; here turn right along a much narrower footpath through bracken, and, in about 5 yards, turn left and come to the corner of a large field. Keep straight on along a headland path beside a newly planted hedge on the left. At the far side of the field, join a cart track that, after dipping slightly into a small valley, continues beside a hedge on the left and meets a road opposite Dale Farm.

7 Turn right along the road. In ¼ mile, turn left along a road signed 'Wantisden church only'. As you walk along the road you will see the church on the skyline. Eventually, after a sharp turn to the left, the road ends at the isolated St John's church. (Some may find a seat in the churchyard a convenient place to relax.)

8 From the church, keep straight on along a grassy path, passing some

industrial buildings on the right. Later, this changes to a headland path with a tall fence on the right. (A gravel farm road leads on the right to the site entrance of the former USAF air base, now being redeveloped. Some of the old buildings can still be seen.) Keep straight on along a broad gravel farm track between hedges, passing a pond behind the hedge on the left, and, on the right, the old water tower.

9 Eventually, the gravel farm road passes through a conifer shelter-belt and bends sharp right. Here go straight on, across a field, towards the middle of a gap in the shelter-belt on the far side of the field. Go through the gap, and continue straight on, still along a cross-field path, towards a large low shed in the distance.

10 At the far side of the field, reach a road and turn left. In 300 yards, join the road from Tunstall coming in from the left, and, in a further 100 yards or so, turn right at Wantisden Corner to walk into Butley and back to the start.

Place of Interest

Orford is 5 miles from Butley. At the centre of this picturesque village stands **Orford Castle** (English Heritage), a 12th century keep and bailey castle, of which the impressive and uniquely designed stone keep and fragments of the foundations now remain. An information board gives details of its original layout and extent. Telephone 01394 450472.

Date walk completed:

....

The Dolphin

The seaside village of Thorpeness is unusual in that the whole village was built as a holiday resort in the early 20th century. The Meare with its creeks and islands was constructed at the same time for boating. The walk crosses The North Warren National Nature Reserve and follows part of a former railway line before returning along the North Sea shore.

The Dolphin is a modern pub, having been rebuilt in 1998 following a fire. The spacious bar and dining area opens onto a paved terrace, where meals are served under an awning. Beyond the terrace is an extensive lawn dotted with picnic tables. The menu, which has several well-known favourites, also includes more unusual fare such as seafood casserole Fearilletta. In addition, a range of tasty 'lite bites' is on offer.

Distance: 4½ miles

OS Explorer 212 Woodbridge and Saxmundham
GR 472598

Good paths and a long board walk across a marsh

Starting point: The Dolphin.

How to get there: From the A12 (Ipswich to Lowestoft) road, take the A1094 to Aldeburgh. Turn left along the coast road for about a mile to reach Thorpeness, where, almost opposite The Meare, there is a pay-and-display car park by the beach.

Opening times are from 11 am to 2.30 pm and 6 pm to 11 pm, Monday to Friday; 11 am to 3 pm and 6 pm to 11 pm on Saturday; and from noon to 3 pm and 6 pm to 10 pm on Sunday. Food is served from noon to 2 pm and 7 pm to 9.30 pm, Monday to Friday; from noon to 2.30 pm and from 7 pm to 10 pm on Saturday; and from noon to 2.30 pm and from 6.30 pm to 8.30 pm on Sunday.

Telephone: 01728 454994.

The Walk

1 From the Dolphin, turn left along the road for about 150 yards, and turn right along Uplands Road, a gravel track signed to Thorpeness windmill. On the right you pass the House in the Clouds, a local landmark, and, almost opposite, the windmill, before joining a surfaced drive from the golf club car park.

2 In 10 yards, where the drive bends left, keep straight on along a narrow footpath. The path leads down through some trees and before long you come out at the edge of the golf course, with The Meare to the left. Beyond the golf course, the path continues between bracken and shrubs, and soon after passing Mere House (1882) reaches Sheepwash Crossing.

3 Cross the former track and continue along a footpath beside a ranch-style fence on the left. Very soon you will be walking through woodland. Using the boardwalk, cross the marshy ground and continue. At a way-marked junction of paths, bear slightly left along the more heavily used path.

4 Join a gravel track and pass to the left a pair of brick houses with flint cobble facing. About 100 yards beyond the houses, turn left at a footpath sign along

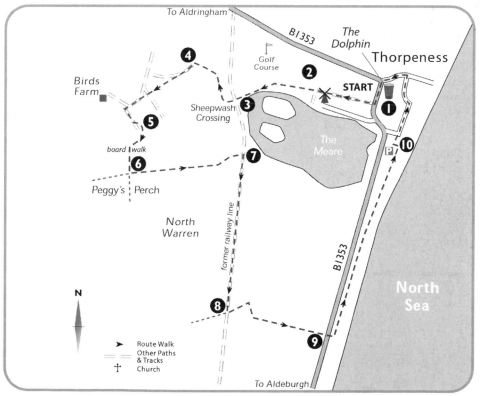

a narrow path through an oak wood. After crossing over a minor track, you come out at a sandy lane. Turn left here and immediately follow the lane round to the right, passing on the left several dwellings and, later, Pantiles, a large house, its gate flanked with eagles. Keeping beside Pantiles' fence, bend left at the corner. Soon the cart track reduces to a narrow footpath that drops down through a wooded area.

5 Go through a barrier fence and follow a boardwalk through part of the RSPB's North Warren Nature Reserve. Cross a long wooden footbridge over a stream and continue through the marshy area along the boardwalk.

6 Just beyond the end of the timber walkway, turn left at a junction of paths. Now follow the Sandlings Path along a grass track through heathland, passing occasional trees and shrubs. Eventually enter an oak wood and join a broader gravel path coming in from the right. Go left along it. The black waymark with the nightjar logo indicates that you are still following the Sandlings Path.

7 At a point where the Sandlings Path bends left, signed to Thorpeness, swing right in the direction of Aldeburgh; cross a stile and join a permissive path along the former railway line.

8 In just over half a mile, pass beside a metal gate to reach a narrow footpath crossing the old railway track. Turn left and in about 10 yards cross a stile. Continue along a grass path between fences. (In the distance, half left, you can see the House in the Clouds.) The path bends right between bushes and later

gradually loops left beside a hawthorn hedge on the left. After a barrier fence the footpath continues on a slightly raised bank between ditches. At the next barrier fence you leave the nature reserve.

9 At the road, cross over, and, in a few yards, turn left along a surfaced footpath. Where the tarmac ends, continue on a path across the grass, going to the right-hand side of the cream house. Continue along the edge of the beach, at first with a fence on your left. On the left look out for and pass a timber walkway leading towards the car park; soon after, pass a sign reading 'No dogs beyond this point'. In a few yards turn left and leave the beach along another walkway, with a platform and seat at its start.

10 Leave the boardwalk. Straight ahead is the Thorpeness pay-and-display car park. To return to the Dolphin, turn right and walk up the Benthills, a surfaced road with the sea on the right. Pass Thorpeness Country Club on the left, and continue along the road. Do not fork right but keep to the wider road. Pass the church on the right and at the end of Church Road turn left back to the Dolphin.

Place of Interest
Snape Maltings, about 5 miles south of Thorpeness, is a complex of 19th century granaries and malthouses. The concert hall is the venue in June of the annual Aldeburgh Festival, developed by the composer Benjamin Britten. There are also shops, a café, craft centre and art gallery.

Date walk completed:
....

The Heron

This varied walk gives a good impression of the Fens' long battle against the threat from water. Since the time of the first sluice, built at nearby Denver in 1651 by a Dutch engineer named Vermuyden, the fight has continued into modern times with the impressive Great Ouse Relief Channel, completed as recently as 1964. Before an

exhilarating final stretch between channel and river on the long-distance Fen Rivers Way, the walk passes along pleasant green footpaths, through the Norman village of Wimbotsham with its gingerbread-brown cottages, and around the fringes of Downham Market.

Distance: 5½ miles

OS Landranger 143 Ely and Wisbech or OS Explorer 236 King's Lynn
GR 604070

An easy, flat walk that can be muddy in places

Starting point: The car park opposite the Heron pub, Stowbridge.

How to get there: Turn left off the A10 two miles north of Downham Market, signed Stowbridge. Cross the Great Ouse Relief Channel, and the car park is immediately on your left.

The Heron is a century-old farmhouse that became a pub some 30 years ago. In its beamed main bar are interesting photographs of sailing boats and the building of the bridge. The food is mainly traditional – steaks, ham or sausage and eggs – with fish dishes such as seafood platter, vegetarian choices, and a range of sandwiches and jacket potatoes. At least five real ales include Woodforde's Wherry and Nog, Adnams Best and Greene King's IPA.

Opening times are noon to 11 pm from Tuesday to Saturday; and noon to 10.30 pm on Sunday. The pub is closed on Mondays. Food is served from noon to 2 pm and from 6 pm to 9 pm from Tuesday to Sunday.

Telephone: 01366 384147.

The Walk

1 Facing the pub, turn right and cross the road bridge over the Great Ouse Relief Channel. Immediately after the bridge, turn right through a wooden gate with a yellow arrow onto a grassy path alongside the water. After about 500 yards, where the path ahead is unofficial and becomes much narrower, head diagonally left up the bank towards the railway line. The turn is not too clearly defined, but when you turn right at the top of the bank you will see ahead of you, across the railway line, a group of buildings and caravans that you are aiming for. After a few yards, head left down the bank to a white gate and cross with care. At the other side continue ahead on a track that leads at first past a caravan settlement and then broadens, with farmland to the left and woodland to the right. Ignore paths to the right, and, where the track meets a road, cross and go ahead on a broad, grassy path.

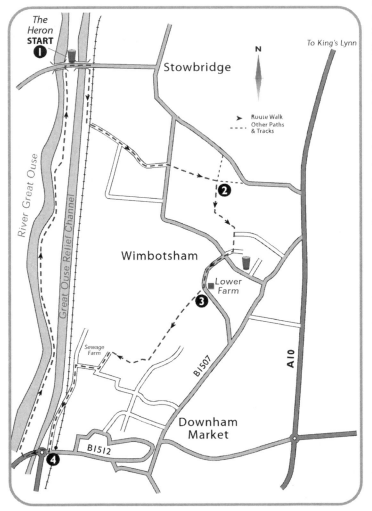

2 At a junction of paths, take the right turn marked with a green Norfolk County Council circular walks arrow and a blue bridleway arrow. Keep straight on, ignoring a path to the right, and where your path meets a gravel track by modern bungalows, turn left over a stile, following a yellow public footpath marker. The narrow path with a wooden fence on the left soon crosses another stile, passes through a field, where there may be a couple of horses, and continues over a third stile and across a meadow to a fourth. Climb over this and at the green arrow turn right. Then keep ahead as the path joins a track to pass bungalows to the left. Keep straight ahead as the lane meets the main road in Wimbotsham. Cross Church Road onto Low Road, passing the village hall on your right.

The River Great Ouse near Stowbridge

3 After about 400 yards, as the road bends left, turn right opposite Lower Farm, following a footpath fingerpost onto a broad path between arable fields. The path bends left, with woodland now on the right – ignore a path to the right – and heads towards modern bungalows. Walk on, with a hedge now on the left and meadowland to the right, and cross a wooden plank bridge with houses to your left. At a T-junction of paths, turn right onto a broader, grassy path which runs alongside garden fences to the left. As the houses end, continue in the direction of a public footpath arrow on a stone marker across rough grassland, through a gap in a hedge, and straight across the next field. At a T-junction by a hedgeline, turn left onto a narrower path which may be slightly overgrown and after 200 yards turn right onto a broader, unsigned track, following a wire fence on your right. Stay on the concrete track, passing a sewage farm to the right, and at a T-junction turn left, still on concrete track, which now runs parallel to the railway line. The track bends right to a gated crossing point, where you go over the London line again. Turn left and go past factory units to meet the main road in Downham Market.

4 Turn right and cross the bridge over the relief channel, following the road round to the left. After 50 yards, turn right at a fingerpost by Linden House. Go up a grassy bank and turn right alongside the River Great Ouse. Cross a stile with a Fen Rivers Way marker and stay on this good, broad path for the next 2½ miles. When the path meets the road, go through double gates and turn right to get back to the pub.

Place of Interest

The Wildfowl and Wetlands Trust reserve at Welney, 6½ miles south of Stowbridge, is famous for its huge flocks of wild swans (Bewick's and whooper) in winter, when there is floodlit viewing. It is also well worth a visit at other times too for a variety of birds and dragonflies. Telephone: 01353 860711.

Date walk completed:

....

The Sandboy

This walk heads out and back through Bawsey Country Park, with its attractive setting of flooded disused sandpits, somewhat surreally equipped with a beach in some cases. Unusual wildflowers, including orchids, thrive here, and there is also a rich variety of birdlife. Good stretches of field path follow, with a visit to the lovely little church of All Saints at Ashwicken – known as 'the church in the fields' – with its unusual 14th century tower.

Distance: 4 miles

OS Landranger 132 North West Norfolk or
OS Explorer 236 King's Lynn
GR 675198

A moderate, mainly flat, walk with
some slopes

Starting point: The public car park at Bawsey Country Park.

How to get there: From the A149 King's Lynn eastern bypass, take the B1145 signed to Gayton. After about a mile, pass The Sandboy pub on the left, and after a further 500 yards turn right into the car park under a height-restriction arch.

The Sandboy is a handsome redbrick Edwardian pub. It owes its present name – it was once known as The Railway – to its setting opposite old sand workings. The pub has been tastefully renovated with a farmhouse-style interior, and food is in traditional English pub style with such dishes as braised beef shank. Fresh fish is also an attraction, and vegetarians are well catered for. Real ales are usually Greene King's IPA and Fuller's London Pride, plus a guest.

Opening times are from noon to 11 pm every day. Food is served from noon to 3 pm and from 6 pm to 9 pm every day.

Telephone: 01553 630527.

The Walk

1 With your back to the road, head diagonally left out of the car park across a grassy area and take a path with a 'no swimming' sign at its entrance. Soon this opens out into a large sandbowl, where signs are lacking, but about halfway into the clearing, turn sharp right up the sand slope towards a wire fence. At the top, turn right onto a path coming in from the left, and after 20 yards fork left alongside the wire fence skirting a lake below to your left. For a good ¼ mile now the path stays close to this fence, a useful marker, as you head up a slope and downhill again, with an open grassy area to the right. At the foot of the slope, take the first path to the left, just before a wider

path comes in from the right. It immediately bends left between trees and, after 20 yards, opens out, with the wire fence again to your left. Where the fence turns sharp left, take the left fork to stay close to it, ignoring a path heading uphill to the right. The path soon opens out into a clearing. Head diagonally right across the clearing and turn left down wooden-edged steps to meet a broad, sandy track. Turn left here, towards the lake. Turn right alongside the fence, and go up steps and over a stile. After 30 yards, the path opens; turn left and head clockwise around a group of young trees. At the other side of this circle, turn sharp left on a narrow path through trees, which leads after 25 yards through an opening in a wire fence onto a broad track.

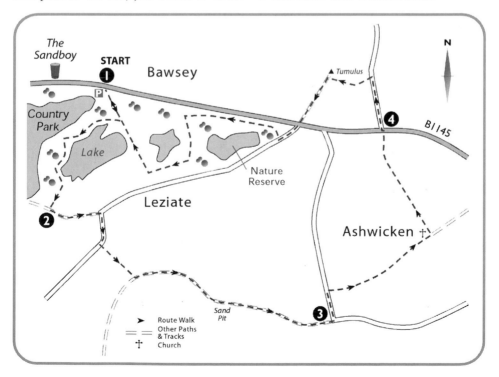

2 Turn left. Soon you pass a sand quarry to the right; then go through an opening in the fence on your right and turn left on a grassy path alongside the track. Take the first opening in the fence you come to, back onto the track, and continue ahead for 20 yards to meet Station Road at Leziate. Cross and turn right and then left onto Holthouse Lane. Continue ahead as the lane becomes unmetalled with open farmland to the left. Where there is a fork in the track by an old horse chestnut tree, head left, following a bridleway fingerpost. Go past more quarry workings and through a wooded area to meet the elbow of a road.

3 Turn left here, and, after about 400 yards, turn right immediately before number 67 onto a grassy path with a not-too-obvious footpath fingerpost in vegetation to the right. Continue in the direction of the Norfolk County Council yellow arrow as this pleasant path heads up a slope with arable fields to the right. Turn left and immediately right at yellow arrows along the field-edge, with the hedge now on your right. The path becomes broader towards a church with a tower. Turn left across a clearing to enter the beautiful little churchyard of All Saints. Skirt the church anti-clockwise and go out through an iron gate onto a broad driveway. Walk ahead for 20 yards and then turn sharp left through a gate with a fingerpost onto a narrow path beyond the church. When this meets a broader path, turn right between cultivated fields and follow the path as it bends left and right to skirt woodland before leading through a hedge and across a plank bridge. The path soon bends left to meet the B1145.

4 Cross the main road and head up Leziate Drove. After the first bungalow on the left, turn left at a bridleway fingerpost (again somewhat hidden) onto a broad track. Where this bends right into a field, head diagonally left across a grassy area and follow a path with electricity cables overhead. At a T-junction, turn left towards the B1145 again. Cross at Brow of the Hill, where the village sign for Leziate and Ashwicken stands, onto the minor road, and after about 200 yards turn right at a footpath fingerpost. The path bends left to run for a good distance parallel to the B1145 and then turns sharply left at a yellow arrow, soon passing a lake to the left, which is a conservation area. Pass a small brick building on the left, and, after 70 yards, turn right away from the wire fence and go downhill for 10 yards to meet a path coming in from the right. Turn left on the path, which leads uphill and stays close to trees on your right. The path then bends right between bracken and soon has garden hedges on the left. At a T-junction of paths, turn right on a broader, grassy path. A lake is visible through trees, and soon you have a clear view of it below to your right. At this point turn left downhill into the sandbowl you were in earlier; keep ahead to return to the car park.

Place of Interest
King's Lynn, 3 miles from Bawsey, is an ancient seafaring town with a rich history. The tourist information centre in the Custom House on Purfleet Quay has leaflets to guide you. Telephone: 01553 763044.

Date walk completed:
....

The Red Lion

This walk leads first through the ancient village of Hockwold (the rest of the name is usually dropped) before setting off on a long straight stretch through open farmland. The return leg then provides fine compensation for earlier efforts, as the path runs alongside the tranquil River Little Ouse for almost the whole of the return

journey. The river forms the meandering boundary between Norfolk and Suffolk, and it is well worth taking binoculars for the wide variety of birds on display.

Distance: *6½ miles*

OS Landranger 143 Ely and Wisbech or OS Explorer 228 March and Ely
GR 735881

A moderately difficult walk, generally flat, but with little shade and the river path is narrowed by vegetation

Starting point: The Red Lion car park, but phone beforehand.

How to get there: Hockwold is 3 miles west of Brandon. From there, take the A1065 north, fork left onto the B1106 just beyond the railway line, and then turn left on a minor road at Weeting. The pub is on the left in the village centre, by a small green.

Over 300 years old, the **Red Lion** is a traditional flint pub with a comfortable rustic feel. Parts of it have been used as a smithy and a coffin store in the past. The extensive menu features steaks (including a 32 oz whopper), though vegetarians are also well catered for. Typical dishes include pan-fried pork fillet, chilli and lemon baked cod, and goat's cheese stuffed aubergine. The regular real ale is Greene King's IPA, with two guests always available.

Opening times are from noon to 2.30 pm and from 6 pm to 11 pm, Monday to Friday; all day from noon on Saturday and Sunday. Food is served from noon to 2.30 pm and from 6.30 pm to 9 pm from Monday to Saturday, and from noon to 9 pm on Sunday.

Telephone: 01842 828875.

99

The Walk

1 Turn right out of the pub car park and left after a few yards onto Main Street, soon passing the church on your left. Stay on this road through the village, passing the school, and keep ahead as it becomes Malts Lane. Go past the post office to the junction with the B1112. Cross onto Burdock Lane and stay on this shady, hedge-lined lane until it bends right by a cottage; here you turn left onto a track, following a bridleway fingerpost. The track bends left over a river. Follow the sandy track as it bends right through attractive, tree-dotted farmland, and, after about ½ mile, turn sharp left at a white Norfolk County Council bridle route arrow on a blue background. Pass fishing lakes to your right to arrive at a T-junction.

2 Turn right onto the broad track of Cowle's Drove. The next mile is generally straight between cultivated fields, with not

much in the way of landscape features. The track veers left and narrows slightly. Then, after another straight half-mile, it bends sharply left across a dyke at the point where a public footpath sign points back the way you have come. After 200 yards, where the track bends right, turn sharp left at a bridle route arrow and go through two narrow metal gates close to each other. Then go immediately right up the bank to the River Little Ouse.

3 Turn left onto a narrow path along the top of the bank, which you follow almost the whole way back. Vegetation can make the going slightly tricky in places, but this is a truly delightful path, raised above the farmland stretching away to the left and with the slow-moving river meandering to the right. (Birdlife in particular is abundant in the ditches and on frequent stretches of open water between the path and the river. Grey herons are almost a certainty; ducks take off steeply as you pass; and the wheezy song of sedge

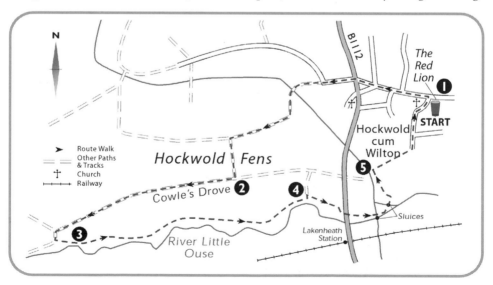

The tranquil Little Ouse river near Hockwold

warblers is everywhere in early summer.) Stay on this elevated path for 2½ miles, turning left down the bank, through a metal gate, and back up again where a wire fence cuts across in three places. A much larger stretch of wildfowl-filled water appears on your right now, across which is the RSPB's new Lakenheath reserve with its distinctive stands of poplars.

4 Just after this open water ends, turn left down the bank and immediately sharp right between fences with wooden rails. Go through a metal gate and ahead on a grassier path, which bends right. Just before the B1112, ignore the white arrow and metal gates to your left (the path is badly overgrown) and go down the bank to your right and through a gate to the road. Cross and go straight ahead at a bridleway fingerpost. Climb over a stile and onto a broad grassy bank, soon to arrive alongside the river again. Keep on the top of the bank and go over a stile/

seat to Hockwold sluice at a junction of waterways. Soon go over a second sluice and turn immediately left on the track with a 'diverted footpath' arrow.

5 After a short stretch, push your way through a large revolving metal gate and then turn immediately right on a broad unsigned track. After about 400 yards, turn left at a T-junction on a track that soon becomes metalled. Go straight on past the church and back to the pub.

Place of Interest
Grime's Graves (English Heritage), 5 miles from Hockwold, between Brandon and Mundford, is a fascinating group of Neolithic flint mines around 4,000 years old. Telephone: 01842 810656.

Date walk completed:
....

101

The Sculthorpe Mill

This is a lovely walk taking in peaceful villages and wildflower-rich meadowland close to the River Wensum. En route you pass Raynham Hall, which has been the home of the Townshend family for centuries, among them Charles 'Turnip' Townshend. He was a politician and agricultural reformer who introduced the turnip from Holland in 1730 to feed cattle through the winter and was a pioneer of crop rotation.

Sculthorpe Mill is in a delightful setting by the Wensum. Built in the 18th century, it has a heavily beamed interior full of character and outside a beautifully planted garden. A lunchtime menu offers sandwiches, jacket potatoes and salads, while a daily specials board has dishes such as spicy sausage and bacon pasta, as well as fish and vegetarian choices. In the evening there is a wider à la carte menu. Regular real ales are Greene King's IPA and Old Speckled Hen.

Opening times are from 11 am to 3 pm and from 6 pm to 11 pm, Monday to Friday; from 11 am to 11 pm on Saturday; and from noon to 4 pm and 6 pm to 11 pm on Sunday. Food is served from noon to 2.30 pm and from 6.30 pm to 9.30 pm.

Telephone: 01328 856161

Distance: *3 miles*

OS Landranger 132 North West Norfolk or OS Explorer 238 East Dereham and Aylsham
GR869265

An easy, flat walk with thick vegetation in places (shorts not advised).

Starting point: Park in the road by the church in Helhoughton or in the first few yards of Park Lane opposite the church.

How to get there: From Fakenham, join the A1065 towards Swaffham. Just after Hempton, turn right on a minor road signed Helhoughton. The church is on your right as you enter the village. To get to the Sculthorpe Mill, take the minor road signed Tatterford, opposite Park Lane in Helhoughton; fork right there through Dunton to join the A148 towards Fakenham. Take the first turn right, where the pub is signed.

The Walk

1 Opposite the church, take the unsurfaced lane signed Park Lane, following a public footpath fingerpost and green Norfolk County Council circular walks arrow. Pass flint-built cottages on your right, and, after about 100 yards, turn left by a yellow arrow into meadowland. Walk ahead for a few yards and then turn right onto a broad, grassy path that runs parallel to the lane. Stay on this pleasant path, soon with a hedge on the right, as it bends left by a green arrow, ignoring a turn to the right. The path narrows as it heads into damp woodland with tall poplar trees to your left and soon crosses the River Wensum, which rises only a couple of miles away to set off on its meandering course to Norwich.

2 Go through a metal gate, still with a green arrow sign, and walk on for a few yards. Turn right on a track heading along a field towards farm buildings. After another metal gate, head through the farmyard as the track bends left and over a cattle grid into parkland, with a church ahead of you. After a few yards, you will see a lake to your right, and, to your left, the grand façade of Raynham Hall in its commanding position at the head of an avenue of trees. It is well worth a detour here into St Mary's church to admire the fine knapped flintwork on its porch and its simple interior, where there are memorials for the Townshends, distinguished soldiers and politicians, from as long ago as 1463. Keeping the church on your left, head out of the park over a cattle grid to a lane.

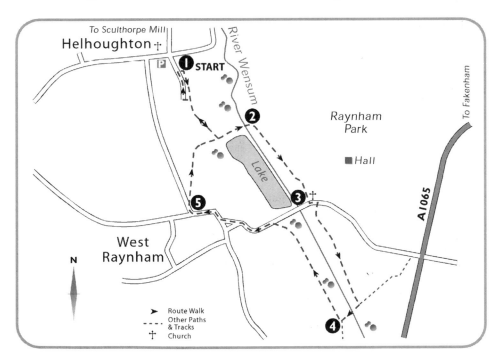

N

	Route Walk
- - - -	Other Paths & Tracks
†	Church

3 Turn left along the lane. After 15 yards, turn right at a footpath fingerpost and green arrow onto a narrow path between trees that soon bends right and left into open meadowland. The going can be made slightly difficult here by thick vegetation, but this is a pleasant path, edged with wildflowers. Woodland is off to your right now, and arable fields rise to the skyline on your left. Shortly after the trees recede, the path turns right and soon crosses a clear stream – the Wensum again – on a plank bridge with a metal handrail.

4 After a second wooden bridge, go over a stile and turn right by a green arrow, ignoring a path heading left. The woodland is now on your right as you go over another stile and a wooden bridge and head along a field edge with rolling farmland away to the left. A further bridge and stile combination, also with a green arrow, takes you onto a path heading diagonally up the meadow and running parallel with the edge of the woodland. Soon there is a glimpse of St Mary's church through the trees. Then the path meets a lane, where you turn left. Stay on the lane up a gentle slope before it bends sharply right into West Raynham. Fork right by the village sign (depicting Townshend's turnips and crop rotation), and after 50 yards right again onto The Street. Pass the village hall on your right and then, as the road bends left, the ruins of St Margaret's church. The former Greyhound pub, now the Old Ale

An imposing view of Raynham Hall

House, is on the right. Shortly after a playground, follow the road as it turns right, signed to Helhoughton.

5 After 50 yards, turn right and follow a footpath fingerpost diagonally left on a clear path cut through a cultivated field, heading for a single tree at the right-hand edge of a copse. At the field's end go ahead for a few yards, with the copse on your left, and then turn right and almost immediately left onto the path you came down early in the walk. (An alternative path shown on the map that goes straight ahead at the copse is missing.) You can either stay on the path and then go onto Park Lane, where you joined it earlier, or, for a slight variation, turn left over a stile and right as soon as the lane begins, to go back to the start.

Date walk completed:

....

Place of Interest

Pensthorpe Nature Reserve and Gardens is 6 miles from Helhoughton, signed off the A1067 south-east of Fakenham. Former gravel pits have been turned into 500 acres of excellently laid out nature trails and lakes with hides and a millennium garden. There is a good visitor centre with a coffee shop and café. Telephone: 01328 851465.

The Three Swallows

take you down to a birdwatcher's delight beside reed-fringed pools and a stretch of shoreline before you head back to the ancient village of Cley, no longer *next the sea*, but attractive nonetheless.

The **Three Swallows** is a great name for a pub (even if it doesn't refer to sinking a pint after a good walk) in this bird-rich part of

This exhilarating walk leads up through rolling wooded farmland to the edge of Salthouse Heath. You will have the opportunity to enjoy a stunning view of sea and grazing marsh spreading out below you. Good paths Norfolk. Formed from three 17th century cottages, its small rooms with panelled walls have a homely atmosphere. The food includes traditional pub fare such as 'Sunday roasts every day', as well as more unusual dishes such as venison in red wine and several vegetarian options. There are usually three cask ales: Adnams best bitter, Greene King's IPA and Abbot.

Opening times (April to October) are from 11 am to 11 pm, Monday to Saturday, and noon to 10.30 pm Sunday; (November to March) from 11 am to 3 pm and 5.30 pm to11 pm, Monday to Friday; all day Saturday and Sunday. Food is served from noon to 2 pm and from 6 pm to 9 pm, Monday to Friday; and from noon to 9 pm on Saturday and Sunday.

Telephone: 01263 740526.

Distance: *4 or 5¾ miles*

OS Landranger 133 North East Norfolk or OS Explorer 251 Norfolk Coast Central GR 048432

A moderate walk with some slopes and a stretch of shingle bank

Starting point: The green opposite the pub.

How to get there: Cley is on the A149, 8 miles west of Sheringham. As you enter the village from the east, take the minor road left, signed 'Newgate', and then turn right at the T-junction; the pub is on the right, just past the church.

The Walk

1 Facing the pub, turn right up the road, soon passing St Margaret's church on your left. The road climbs gradually, passing Old Woman's Lane on the left. After a further 150 yards, turn right at a public footpath fingerpost alongside a campsite entrance and walk up a flinty track hedged on both sides. At the top of the slope the path opens out on the right to give an excellent view, taking in three churches: Blakeney, Wiveton and Cley. Soon cross a metalled lane and continue on a path (with fingerpost) up a sloping field-edge. Beyond the field, the path twists through an area of bracken and bramble and then progresses downhill through light woodland to emerge alongside farmland. Walk up a slope, through a gap in a hedge, and straight ahead to meet the elbow of a road.

2 Turn left here, following a fingerpost up a hedged grassy path, which levels out with farmland to the left. Stay ahead as the path broadens into a track and leads downhill to meet a road. Cross the road into a minor road signed 'Salthouse and Kelling', which bends left through

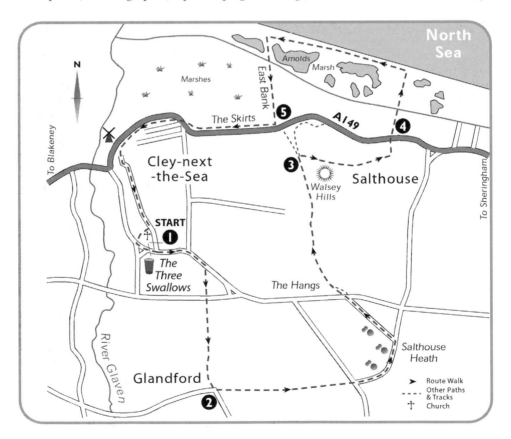

attractive woodland. At the first crossroads, turn left, still with woodland on both sides. Immediately before a T-junction, head diagonally right across a patch of grass and cross the road to take a footpath, signed to Walsey Hills, with a green Coast Path Circular Walks arrow. There is a short stretch up a slope and at the brow of the hill a splendid view is suddenly spread out before you. Stay with this path as it heads downhill.

❸ As you reach the bottom of a long field immediately before a wooded area, turn right at a green arrow and fingerpost signed to Salthouse. *To shorten the walk, keep straight ahead here to meet the busy A149, turn left on the road for a short distance, and pick up the walk at point 5.* After 20 yards, at the end of the copse of low trees, ignore a path turning sharply left and keep ahead on a clear path that leads up through an arable field. At the brow of the hill you have more fine views across the marshes. Walk along a field edge, with a hedge to your right, cross a track and go through a gap in a hedge. The path then bends left down a sloping field under cultivation. At the field's end, walk on in the direction of the green arrow; after 10 yards turn left, ignoring a path uphill to the right, and head down to the A149.

❹ Cross the road and take a broad grassy path that goes over the dyke on a brick bridge and heads straight for the sea-defence bank in the distance. The sea is hidden as you walk alongside reed-fringed pools, but soon comes into view as you head up the bank and turn left onto the shingle North Norfolk Coast Path. The going here is not easy underfoot but the reward is enormous. After just over half a mile of exhilarating walking, take the first path down the slope and continue along the East Bank, a mecca for birdwatchers.

❺ Just before arriving at the A149, turn right down the bank, passing a small car park, to reach a grassy path running parallel to the road. Continue past a couple of openings into the reserve to the right as the path becomes a boardwalk that soon meets the road. After 50 yards, pass a road signed 'Newgate' to the left and cross the main road to take a raised footpath that leads in front of houses. Go ahead as this runs into the road and past shops. Opposite a sign to the windmill, turn left through a brick arch onto an alleyway between cottages. Pass a small car park and turn left at a T-junction and right alongside the former school. The path meets a road, where you head right. *(After a few yards, there is a fingerposted detour, down an alley to the right to Cley's main street).* Otherwise stay ahead as the road narrows to become Church Lane, passing houses on both sides and allotments on the left. Then turn right at a green arrow and a sign to St Margaret's church. Go into the churchyard and turn right down a narrow path alongside the pub's beer garden to meet the road and pub to your left.

Place of Interest

Cley Marshes bird reserve is set among reedbeds and dotted with lakes. There is a visitor centre just east of the village by the A149. Telephone: 01263 74008.

Date walk completed:

....

The Gamekeeper

tarting in the delightful village of Old Buckenham with its huge – one of the country's largest – wildflower-dotted green, this varied walk heads past an old windmill and then takes in shady tracks and lanes, open farmland and pasture before skirting New Buckenham and its castle, rich in history.

Distance: *5 miles*

OS Landranger 144 Thetford and Diss or OS Explorers 237 and 230
GR 064916

An easy, flat walk

Starting point: The car park of the Gamekeeper in Old Buckenham, but phone beforehand.

How to get there: From Attleborough, take the B1077 south for 3 miles. The pub is on the right as you enter the village.

The Gamekeeper is a farmhouse-style pub, built in 1639, and its atmospheric interior is divided into cosy rooms with floors of red tiles, stone flags or wood. There are two non-smoking restaurant rooms and an attractive garden. Food is a mixture of traditional English – braised shank of lamb, bangers and mash – and foreign-influenced dishes such as poussin, spatchcock and Mediterranean vegetable and mushroom stroganoff. Real ales come from the Wolf brewery at nearby Attleborough and Adnams of Southwold, with a regular guest.

Opening times are all day from noon. Food is served from noon to 2.30 pm and from 6.30 pm to 9 pm, Monday to Thursday; from noon to 2.30 pm and from 6.30 pm to 9.30 pm on Friday and Saturday; and on Sunday from 12.30 pm to 5 pm.

Telephone: 01953 860397.

The Walk

1 Turn right out of the car park in front of the pub, passing between a row of cottages and a pond. With the green stretching away to your left and ahead, turn right in front of more cottages and cross Forge Close, staying on the gravel path as it bends left to meet the road. Turn right on the pavement. After 100 yards turn left onto a road that leads to a T-junction. Turn right on Mill Road, passing the windmill on the left, and head out of the village on a hedged lane. After 100 yards turn left at a fingerpost and yellow Norfolk County Council arrow onto a grassy track. On meeting a road, turn right. After 200 yards turn left on a road signed 'Wilby and Eccles'. Soon turn left again, still signed to Wilby and Eccles, and after a further 250 yards turn left on Sandy Lane, following a fingerpost.

2 Stay on this broad and pleasant track, lined with tall trees, soon passing the gates of Lodge Farm on your left. Ignore a footpath marked on the map to the right, and, as the track narrows, continue with woodland to the left and views to the right over meadowland. At the end of the track turn left onto Banham Road. After 300 yards, turn right at a public footpath fingerpost and yellow arrow onto a broad path leading between arable fields. Where the main path appears to bend right, stay straight ahead on a narrow path along the left-hand edge of a field. Then continue in the same direction, passing a yellow arrow, with an area of young trees to the right. Follow yellow arrow markers left across a wooden footbridge and

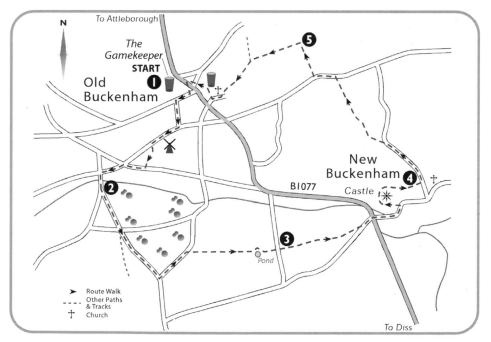

immediately right, with a small pond on your right. After some 20 yards, turn right across a ditch and walk along a field edge, soon with hedge on your right, to meet a road.

3 Cross the road and keep straight ahead, as marked by a fingerpost; go over the first of eight stiles within a fairly short distance. The path becomes broad and grassy, passing low farm sheds to the left. It then narrows between arable fields, eventually swinging right to meet a road. Turn left, and, after a few yards, go straight across the crossroads to New Buckenham Road. Stay on the pavement, following signs to New Buckenham and Norwich. The road swings left; after a few yards, where it bends right, turn sharp left between metal posts onto a path with a fingerpost. Keep to the broad grassy path as it skirts clockwise round the rather sinister looking moat of New Buckenham Castle and passes the tall metal gates of the castle itself, which is screened from view by high earthworks. Stay alongside the moat until the path peels off, bending slightly left and heading for a tall church tower, soon with modern bungalows to your right. Where the path meets a lane, the village of New Buckenham is to your right; here there is a shop and two pubs for refreshments.

4 The route, however, goes left on Cuffer Lane, soon passing a cemetery on the right. Where the lane bends sharply right, turn left at a fingerpost and green Tas Valley Way arrow. Go over a stile. The path bends diagonally right across a field, passes through a metal gate, and bends right again, still with the Tas Valley marker, between crops. This is another attractive stretch of footpath through open farmland, soon passing a small pond and crossing a plank bridge. When the path meets a narrow lane, turn left. After about 250 yards, opposite the large farm buildings of Old Hall, turn right at a Tas Valley marker onto a broad track.

5 After a further 250 yards, turn left by a public footpath fingerpost (hidden in the hedge) and a green circular walks arrow onto a narrower path with a ditch on the left. Cross a wooden bridge with a handrail and go over a stile, the first of several with a lift-up top rail. Go diagonally left across a field in which docile horses and foals from Old Buckenham Stud graze. Cross over a stile, turn left onto a track, and, almost immediately, turn right through a fence. Cross the field, where there are more horses, go over another stile, and turn left into the churchyard. Turn right to All Saints' church and follow the path to the church entrance. Turn right onto the lane, and, opposite the Ox and Plough pub, head diagonally right on a grassy path across the village green. Cross the road to the start.

Place of Interest
New Buckenham, 1½ miles from Old Buckenham, is unique in England as a medieval planned town. It was built after the castle was established by the Normans in 1145, and is well worth a walk round. The key to the castle grounds is available from Castle Hill Garage. St Martin's church is an impressive, light and airy building dating from the mid-13th century.

Date walk completed:
....

The Ugly Bug Inn

attractive fringes of a golf course before the path heads across grassland full of wild flowers and through two lovely stretches of woodland. The walk then returns through the village, passing a superb red-brick barn bearing the date 1666.

There is a fine mix of landscapes on this short walk, much of it in the valley of the infant River Yare. Quiet country lanes give way to the

The Ugly Bug Inn is a family-run pub converted from an old barn. Its cosy, open-plan interior is divided into smaller areas featuring a wealth of old advertising signs. Outside, a patio overlooks a delightful garden with its own lake. The evening menu has dishes such as chef's special meatloaf and prawn korma, while a lighter lunch menu offers a good range of sandwiches and salads. Regular real ales are Woodforde's Wherry, Fuller's London Pride and Greene King's Abbot; in addition, two guests are usually available.

Distance: 3 miles

OS Landranger 144 Thetford and Diss or OS Explorer 237 Norwich
GR 104099

An easy, flat walk with a couple of gentle slopes

Starting point: The pub car park, but phone beforehand.

How to get there: From Norwich take the A47 towards Dereham. After 8 miles turn left on a minor road after the turn for Easton. In Colton, take the road out of the village signed 'E. Tuddenham' and turn left on High House Farm Lane. The pub is on the left, and there is car parking in front of it or across the lane.

Opening times are from noon to 3 pm and from 6 pm to 11 pm, Monday to Thursday, and all day from noon, from Friday to Sunday. Food is served from noon to 2 pm and from 7 pm to 9 pm, except on Sundays when the serving times are 12.30 pm to 3.30 pm.

Telephone: 01603 880794.

The Walk

1 With your back to the pub, turn left into the lane, which soon bends sharply left before passing The Grange on the right. At the T-junction, where to your left you can see the square tower of St Andrew's church, turn right onto Church Lane, signed to Barnham Broom. At first the lane is flanked by tall trees, which soon give way to rolling farmland as it heads up a slope. Where the lane levels, there are good open views between old oaks spaced along the way. The route then goes downhill again.

2 At the bottom, where the lane bends right, turn left onto a track by a public footpath fingerpost. With the golf course of Barnham Broom Hotel on your right, pass a cottage on your left and keep ahead through a wooden gate with a yellow arrow marker. Follow the defined path along a landscaped slope and then over a stile. Head along a field edge, with a hedge on your right. Where the hedge bends right, stay ahead across the field to a yellow Norfolk County Council arrow marker. Go through the hedge, turn right, and, soon after, turn left to skirt the cultivated field.

3 After about 100 yards, turn right onto the golf course through an obvious gap in the hedge. There is, regrettably, no sign before this turn, but as soon as you are through the gap you see a fingerpost directing you left. Follow the low white posts at the edge of the course. After about 100 yards, where the mown grass area bends right, keep straight on along a clear grassy path that soon swings

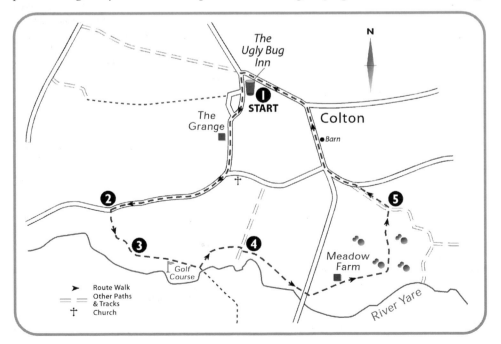

diagonally right across a lovely, unspoilt meadow. (Before heading across this open grassland, there is a bench to the right under a small oak that makes a perfect spot for a rest.) At the point where the path almost touches the river, head diagonally left towards the hedgeline. (Before you do, however, it is worth a detour of a few yards to a wooden bridge over the shallow River Yare. There could scarcely be a greater contrast between the stream at this point and the broad expanse of Breydon Water as it nears the end of its journey to the sea at Yarmouth.) At the hedgeline, the path bends right alongside woodland, with more attractive grassland to the right.

❹ At a T-junction with a broader track, turn right; after 20 yards turn left at a yellow public footpath arrow onto a narrower path that soon heads across a wooden bridge with a handrail and into woodland. The path now broadens as it heads between trees and then goes through a wire fence and out into a wildflower-dotted meadow again. Pass a modern house on the left and go over a stile (with dog-flap) to a lane. Cross this and follow a public footpath fingerpost along a broad track to Meadow Farm. The track leads between a modern house on the left and farm buildings; then, at a yellow arrow, it becomes a narrower path that bends left and immediately right into Colton Wood, another attractive stretch of mixed woodland. The path comes out of the wood and turns left uphill through an open area, soon becoming a clearer track that veers left and right, with trees on both sides, and then open farmland to the left.

❺ At a T-junction turn left onto a

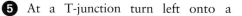

The magnificent barn at Colton has a date of 1666 on it

broader track with good views all round. When this meets a lane turn left, soon passing the Colton sign at the entrance to the village. At a junction of roads, turn right, signed 'E. Tuddenham and Honingham', and head along The Street. Pass a duckpond to your left and a handsome red-brick barn to the right. At the T-junction turn left, signed to East Tuddenham, passing the grounds of Colton Manor House on the left, and head out of the village, taking the next lane to the left, High House Farm Lane, back to the pub.

> **Place of Interest**
> **Norwich**, only 5 miles from Colton, is rich in historical interest; its magnificent Norman cathedral and castle are especially recommended. The Castle Museum and Art Gallery has had an extensive facelift and now has exhibitions devoted to Queen Boudicca and the Viking era. Telephone: 01603 493625.

> **Date walk completed:**
> ....

The Scole Inn

Scole is an attractive village on an old coach route to London. It was plagued for many years by heavy traffic but a bypass has left it much quieter and it makes a good starting point for a walk on green lanes, quiet country roads and open farmland. The route also takes in stretches of two long-distance paths, as well as a secluded church which ranks among the loveliest in this county of fine churches.

Dutch-gabled and wisteria clad, **Scole Inn**, dating back to 1655, is a handsome coaching hotel with an impressive period interior. The bar food consists of traditional pub fare such as steak and Guinness hotpot and lamb shank, together with fish dishes such as baked sea bass and vegetarian options. There is a wider choice in the à la carte restaurant. Regular real ales are Greene King's IPA and Abbot.

Opening times are from 8 am for tea or coffee; alcoholic drinks are served from 11 am to 11 pm every day. Light bites are available from 9 am, and main meals are served between noon and 2.30 pm and from 6.30 pm to 9.30 pm.

Telephone: 01379 740481.

Distance: *4 miles*

OS Landranger 144 Thetford and Diss or OS Explorer 230 Diss and Harleston GR 149789

An easy walk, flat with a couple of gentle slopes.

Starting point: The car park of Scole Inn.

How to get there: Scole is a mile southeast of Diss. From the roundabout at the junction of the A1066 and the A140, follow the road signed to Scole. Turn left at the T-junction; the pub is on the left and the car park is at the end of the long building.

The Walk

❶ Turn right out of the pub car park and pass in front of the pub. Take the first road to the right. At a roundabout in 20 yards, stay on the pavement as it bends right to meet the busy A140. Cross this and immediately turn right on a gravel path, which climbs steadily as it runs parallel to the road. After about 300 yards, go through a wooden fence and turn left. Cross a track and go ahead at a public bridleway fingerpost. You are now on Miller's Lane, a pleasant and shady path where birdsong takes over as the noise of traffic fades. The hedges on both sides give way to open farmland. Continue ahead as the path broadens,

passing a copse on the left and heading towards a group of red-roofed houses. Go under a power line. The path bends right, becoming a gravel track past houses before meeting the bend of a lane.

❷ Turn left on the lane, soon passing farm buildings and the Diss Business Centre on your left. After 100 yards or so, turn right, and, following a public bridleway fingerpost and a blue Norfolk County Council arrow, head along the concrete track towards Frenze Hall. The track is hedged on the left at first and then drops downhill with woodland on both sides. Soon you will see Frenze Hall and a church ahead. Follow the track between the hall and the church. (But I recommend

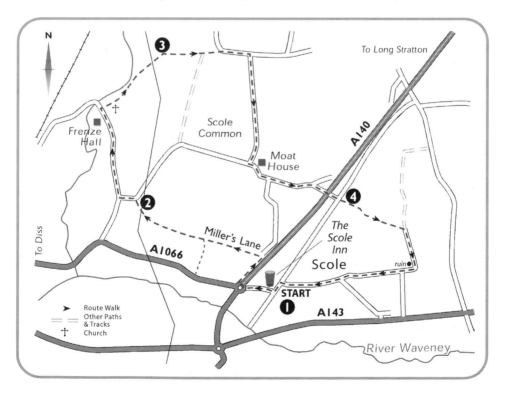

a visit to St Andrew's first. This lovely flint-built church, claimed to be the smallest in Norfolk, has a simple interior that is full of interest. It is no longer used for worship but is well maintained by the Churches Conservation Trust. The key can be had from the hall.) After leaving the church, follow the track as it bends right, ignoring an Angles Way path off to the left. The track then bends left and you leave it to go over a stile by a gate on your left. Go ahead, following a Boudica's Way sword marker along the right-hand field edge. Go under the power line and immediately turn right over a stile, following the sword.

❸ Again there is welcome shade on this pleasant green lane, which soon becomes a tunnel of overarching hedgerows. Continue to follow it as it broadens to become a track. Where it meets the bend of a road, turn right on what is a designated *quiet lane*, as part of a scheme to encourage motorists to drive slowly and respect walkers, cyclists and horseriders using it. After about 300 yards, turn right on Burston Road, signed 'Scole Common'. Heading up a slight slope, you stay on the metalled lane for a longish stretch now, but it is little-used by traffic and the grass verge is walkable in places. Passing the attractive gardens of the Moat House on your left, follow the road as it bends sharp left. Ignore a road and a footpath to the right and soon pass Low Road to your right. Then, after a further 250 yards, the road rises to pass over the A140.

❹ At a T-junction at the end of the bridge turn left and immediately cross the road to head along a footpath with a fingerpost and the first of several Angles Way otter markers. Keep to the field edge. Then, where the hedge ends after about 100 yards, head diagonally right across the cultivated field, following a yellow arrow and Crossfield Path marker. At the far side, turn left alongside the hedge. Turn right at the field's end; then, after 20 yards, turn left into the next field. The direction of the marker here is misleading, as it appears to point you diagonally left across to the far corner, but instead you have to turn sharper left than that to head across towards a metal gate. Go through the gate with a yellow arrow into the next field and then head diagonally right to the far corner. Climb the stile and turn right into a narrow, metalled lane, which you follow as it bends sharply right where the ruins of St Mary's church stand in the field. Where the lane bends sharply left, keep straight on along an unsigned grassy path on the edge of an arable field. Pass a tall-chimneyed hall to the left, and, ignoring a path off to the right, follow the path round to the left to meet a road after a further 50 yards. Turn right on the road into Scole, crossing just before the T-junction to take a path to the left, back to the pub.

Place of Interest

Bressingham Steam Experience and Gardens, 6 miles from Scole on the A1066 west of Diss, has a working steam locomotive collection and Dad's Army display. There are two fine gardens and a large nursery, established by the Bloom family. Telephone: 01379 686900 (or 686903 for a 24-hour information line).

Date walk completed:

....

The Old Red Lion

arts of Norfolk still offer a stride back in time, nowhere more so than Aldborough and its surrounding farmland. In the middle of this lovely village, the green, surrounded by houses with names such as 2nd Slip Cottage and Longstop Cottage, is still the venue for regular cricket matches. The walk confirms this as a genuinely unspoilt corner, with a delightful green lane

giving way to quiet byroads, good grassy paths, and a gem of a church.

The Old Red Lion has an unusual set-up: part of it is a traditional village pub with beamed and brick interior, but through a doorway is a cosy, parlour-style tearoom, all cakes and scones. The food on offer is traditional pub grub such as steak and kidney pie, freshly cooked, with Sunday roasts a speciality. Sandwiches can also be taken away, and walkers can have flasks filled. Real ales are Old Red Lion Bitter and Golden, both from Winters of Norwich, and a couple of guests.

Distance: *4 miles*

OS Landranger 133 North East Norfolk or OS Explorer 252 Norfolk Coast East GR184343

An easy walk, mainly flat with a couple of slight slopes.

Starting point: In front of the Old Red Lion or beside the green at Aldborough.

How to get there: Aldborough is 18 miles north of Norwich, signed left off the A140 between Aylsham and Cromer.

Opening times are from 11 am to 11 pm in summer and from noon to 11 pm in winter. Food is served from noon to 2 pm, but no cooked food is available on Monday and Tuesday lunchtimes. Evening meals are by arrangement; phone the landlady first.

Telephone: 01263 761451.

Walk 37 *Aldborough*

The Walk

1 With your back to the pub, turn right and walk alongside the village green. Keep to Chapel Road as it bends right and left, passing the Methodist chapel on the left. Just after the houses end and the road bends left, turn right onto a plank bridge and cross over a stile, following a yellow public footpath arrow. Head across the meadow and go over a stile by a dyke onto a lane. Turn right on the lane, which bends left and soon passes Aldborough Primary School. Pass Middle Hill Lane on the right and after 25 yards turn left on a track named Alby Hill. After 50 yards, turn right by a yellow arrow and right

again after another 50 yards onto a track that passes Orchard House to your left. The grassy path bends left alongside the garden and soon becomes a pleasant green corridor with overarching hedges and glimpses of open country between.

2 When the path meets a lane, turn right; after 40 yards, turn left at a public footpath fingerpost and walk along the field edge, heading for the square tower of a church. Just before St Ethelbert's church there is a footpath diversion to the right into an old graveyard, which you cross diagonally to come out through a wooden gate into a road. Cross this to head along a narrower road. After 50 yards, turn

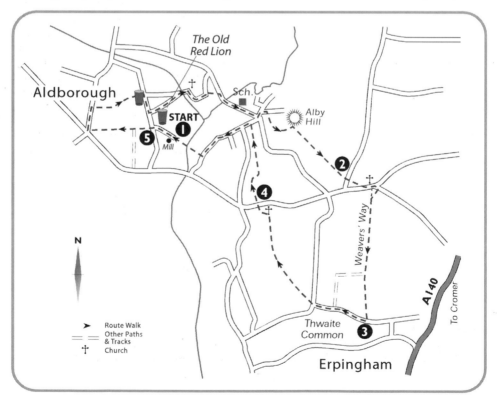

right at a fingerpost (somewhat hidden in the hedge to the left) and cross a concrete yard with a large shed on the right. Stay ahead on the broad path with good views to both sides. Where the main path turns right, continue straight ahead on a path cut through crops. At the end of the field, keep ahead on a grassy path that passes a couple of houses to meet a lane. (There is a slight divergence from the map, which shows a dog-leg here.)

3 Turn right onto the lane, soon passing the former Thwaite School of red brick on your left and several attractive cottages on the right. At the T-junction, take the right-hand slip road and cross onto a footpath with a fingerpost and a Weavers' Way marker. Follow the path cut through a long arable field towards a church tower on the horizon. Continue into the next field, heading straight for the church, with good views to the left. The path turns left and right to skirt the Saxon church of All Saints with its round tower before meeting a road. (A detour into the church is highly recommended.)

4 Turn left on the road, and after 40 yards turn right. Cross over a stile to follow a fingerpost along a field edge, with a hedge on your right. Go through a metal gate, turn immediately right at a Weavers' Way arrow, and, after a few yards, go left along the edge of the meadow, with a wire fence to your right. Continue into the next field, which has been used as a turf farm, and go over a stile to the lane. Turn left on

the lane. (For a shortcut back to the village, however, turn right; then left at the T-junction and retrace your steps past the school.) After passing Home Farm House and several old flint cottages on the left and a bungalow on the right, turn right at a Weavers' Way marker onto a path that crosses a stream (Scarrow Beck) on a concrete bridge. The path bends left on a wooden-railed bridge in front of an old mill that has been converted into houses. Turn right here on a gravel lane that meets the road by a garage. (Again there is a shortcut, by turning right into the village.)

5 Cross the road to go onto a track at a fingerpost. Where the track bends left into a farm, continue ahead on a grassy path that bends right and left to head up a slight slope to the end of a line of trees. Following the direction of a yellow arrow, continue along the end of an orchard and then on a field edge. On meeting a lane, turn right (ignoring the footpath ahead). The lane bends right and then left; here take a grassy marked path to the right and pass between arable fields towards a line of houses. Go between the houses and along Prince Andrew's Close. Turn right in front of the Black Boys pub and then left alongside the village green to reach the Old Red Lion.

Date walk completed:

....

Place of Interest

Felbrigg Hall (National Trust), 3 miles north of Aldborough, is one of the finest 17th century houses in East Anglia. The 1750-acre estate has nature trails, woodland, a walled garden and a tearoom/restaurant. Telephone: 01263 837444.

The White Horse

Horses are a feature of this walk, which passes through a variety of attractive scenery: woodland and open farmland crossed by quiet lanes and broad paths lined with hedges rich in wildlife. The pub at the starting point was the residence of artist Sir Alfred Munnings, who lodged there as a young man in the early 1900s while painting his distinctive landscapes, which often featured horses. The

walk also offers a glimpse of a handsome hall, and, towards the end, follows a footpath alongside the meadows of a large horse sanctuary.

The White Horse is a popular roadside

Distance: *5 miles*

OS Landranger 134 Norwich and the Broads or OS Explorer OL40 The Broads GR 258164

A moderate walk with slight slopes and a muddy section near the beginning.

Starting point: The car park of the White Horse, but phone beforehand.

How to get there: Crostwick is 3 miles north-east of Norwich, on the B1150 North Walsham road. The pub is on the right of the main road, shortly after the village sign.

inn dating back to 1836, if not earlier. It offers a friendly welcome and an extensive menu. Inside, in the beamed bar and restaurant, there are lots of cosy corners decorated with old photographs. Dishes include a range of steaks and homemade pies – beef and Guinness, for example – Norfolk crab salad, and chicken with Stilton. There is a good vegetarian selection and some vegan dishes. Five real ales are always on tap, with Greene King's IPA and Old Speckled Hen the regulars.

Opening times are from 11 am to 11 pm every day. Food is served from 11 am to 9.30 pm, Monday to Saturday, and from 11 am to 9 pm on Sunday.

Telephone: 01603 737560.

The Walk

1 Turn right out of the pub car park and walk on the grass verge alongside the B1150. About 60 yards after going over a river, turn right over a stile, following a public footpath fingerpost; ahead of you is a long, wet meadow, where the going can be slightly tricky after heavy rain. The path sticks closely to the hedge on your left with occasional detours round muddy sections. At the end of the field, go over a stile; after a few yards, cross a second one to emerge in a narrow lane. Turn left and follow this quiet tree-lined road as it climbs gradually and levels out. At the end of a straight stretch (bright with rosehips in early autumn) where the road bends sharply left, turn right,

following a public bridleway fingerpost onto a broad track known as Granny Bard's Lane. I have not been able to discover who Granny was, but she has given her name to a very pleasant path, hedged on the right and with farmland off to the left. Pass a private track on the right and stay ahead as the path narrows and becomes grassier.

2 After a further 200 yards, at the end of the field and just before a wide gap in the hedge through to the next field, the path turns left and runs alongside a hawthorn hedge on your right. It continues along the end of the field and climbs slightly, passing a stretch of woodland and then an arable field on the left. Where the path meets the bend of a road, turn right and

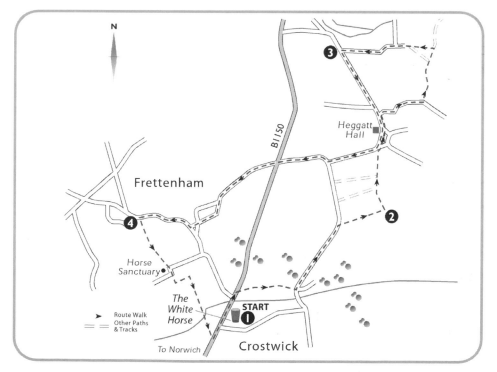

121

follow the road as it bears left, soon passing Heggatt Hall, which can be glimpsed through trees to your left. At a junction of roads turn right onto Heggatt Street, following a bridleway fingerpost. This metalled lane soon becomes a pleasant track as it heads past cottages on the right and then bends sharply left (ignore a path to the right here) up a slope, hedged on both sides. When you reach a metal gate and the path ahead is private, turn left to follow a blue Norfolk County Council bridleway arrow by woodland to your right. Continue ahead, ignoring a path to the left. At a junction of paths, turn left at a blue arrow onto a broader track which leads past open farmland on the right then bends left and right before meeting a road.

❸ At this junction, turn left onto Heggatt Road, a quiet lane. Keep straight ahead, soon retracing a short stretch walked earlier, and then stay on the road to a T-junction. Turn right here onto Caius Heath Lane, which bends left to meet the main road. Cross the busy B1150 and walk down Stanninghall Road, which is hedged at first and then bends left and right, opening out with pleasant views. At a T-junction, take a slip road to the right and turn right on the road signed to Frettenham, which bends left, passing houses on the left.

❹ Just after Warren Cottage, turn left through a wooden gate on a footpath with a yellow arrow (somewhat hidden by vegetation) and fingerpost. Continue beside the extensive meadows of the Redwings Horse Sanctuary with its many animals. Go through another wooden gate and follow a track that leads up a slope and past the sanctuary's

Redwings Horse Sanctuary near Frettenham

headquarters to the right and then passes between meadows with horses on both sides. At the next wooden gate, a yellow arrow (and indeed the OS map) directs you straight ahead down a long field, but a better alternative path has been established. Go through the gate and then turn immediately left; after a few yards, turn right to follow the field edge, keeping the hedge on your left. Where the hedge ends, stay straight ahead across grassland and then pass into a lightly wooded area. Cross a concrete bridge over a stream and continue ahead as the path becomes a track and bends left to meet the B1150. Cross the road and turn left on the grass verge, soon crossing Dow Lane to return to the pub.

Place of Interest

The **City of Norwich Aviation Museum** at Horsham St Faith, 3 miles from Crostwick, has a collection of civil and military aircraft, including a Vulcan bomber, and displays relating to aviation history and the secret work of the RAF 100 Group. Telephone: 01603 893080.

Date walk completed:

....

The Fisherman's Return, Winterton-on-Sea

takes you alongside the attractive River Thurne, where a couple of ancient wind pumps still stand, and at the same time you can see the ten turbines of the West Somerton wind farm. The walk also provides a tantalizing glimpse of Martham Broad.

The 300-year-old **Fisherman's Return** at Winterton has a strong nautical feel, with its wood-panelled walls and old photographs of fishermen and sailing boats. It is a warm and cosy place, with a specials menu on which fish dishes feature strongly, including a popular cheese-and-potato-topped fish pie. Regular real ales are Adnams Best and Broadside and Woodforde's Wherry, with three guests usually on tap. There's a large family room and a good-sized beer garden.

W ind power has long played a key role in Norfolk life, and this walk provides an interesting contrast between old and new. The path

Distance: *4½ miles*

OS Landranger 134 Norwich and the Broads or OS Explorer OL40 The Broads GR 456180

An easy, flat walk with occasional thick vegetation. Shorts not advised

Starting point: The public car park next to the King's Head pub in Martham.

How to get there: Martham is on the B1152, 7 miles north of Great Yarmouth. The car park is in the centre of the village, opposite a large duckpond. To get to Winterton, take the B1152 towards the coast, turn right on the B1159, left into the village following a 'beach' sign, and right on The Lane.

Opening times are from 11 am to 2.30 pm and from 6.30 pm to 11 pm, Monday to Friday; 11 am to 11 pm on Saturday; and from noon to 10.30 pm on Sunday. Food is served from noon to 2 pm and from 6.30 pm to 9 pm.

Telephone: 01493 393305.

123

The Walk

1 Turn right out of the car park to pass in front of the King's Head. After a few yards, the road bends right, past shops, to join Black Street. Pass St Mary the Virgin church on your right and follow the main road as it bends right where a narrower road comes in from the left. Soon pass a school on your right; after 50 yards, turn left over a stile with a Norfolk County Council yellow arrow marker onto a narrow grassy path between houses. Where this meets an arable field, turn right; after 15 yards, go left on a clear path through the field. Follow the path as it leads between fields and then through a

field to meet a track that comes in from the right. Stay ahead for 10 yards and turn left onto a gravel path, keeping a duck pond on your right. (There is a divergence from the OS map here, as the path has been rerouted away from a farmyard and buildings.) The path bends sharp right, over a concrete hardstanding, to meet a track; here you turn left. Where this meets a metalled lane, turn right. Stay on this narrow lane as it bends left then passes a track on the right. After a few more yards, turn right, following a public footpath fingerpost onto a track that immediately bends left to run alongside a strip of water with moored boats. Walk through the small car park of Martham

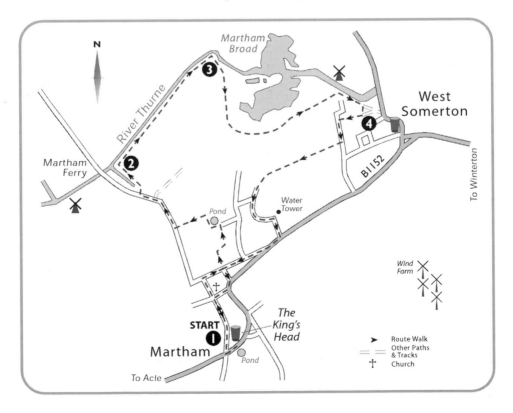

124

Pits fishery and then walk back to the waterway on your left and ahead to the river.

2 Turn right onto the path alongside the River Thurne, which can be seen from time to time through tall reeds on your left. The vegetation can now be thick in places, but it is never bad enough to present a real problem and you have good views over open grazing marsh. (Away to your right you can see a single turbine and, to the left of that, the 10 turbines of the West Somerton wind farm, the first such in Norfolk. Across the river to your left, in contrast, is a derelict wind pump.) Stay on the path as it leaves the riverbank for a few yards and then heads back alongside it.

3 Soon the river and the path turn sharp right. After a few yards, the path leaves the water to head in the direction of the single turbine. Reedbeds now stretch away to your left, and there are occasional glimpses of the open water of Martham Broad. The path bends left to pass between gorse bushes and trees, then through woodland, and finally through a gap in a wooden fence onto a path rich in butterflies and dragonflies. Soon the path takes you up to a waterway again – Somerton Boat Dyke – where you turn right and follow the water until it ends. Continue ahead; after 35 yards go through a wooden gate and turn right at a footpath fingerpost onto a grassy path. (If you wish to make a detour for refreshments at this point, turn left at the gate, go down the track, and then turn right onto the main road for a short distance to reach the Lion pub.)

4 Follow the path as it bends left and

right alongside a garden and a house and meets a narrow metalled lane. Turn left past Rectory Cottage; then, after about 200 yards, turn right at a footpath fingerpost on a broad grassy path along a field edge. On the OS map the path is marked straight ahead here, but you will find that it bends to follow field edges. Stay on the path as bungalows appear on the left; then keep ahead as it becomes a broader track and then the metalled Damgate Back Lane. This passes houses on the left and becomes a track again, bending left and heading up a slope towards a water tower and a line of houses, before turning right to meet a road. Turn right on the B1152; then, after 50 yards, fork right – signed to Martham Staithe – and soon you will find yourself at the place where you took the first footpath between houses. For a slightly different way back, turn left on School Road; then turn right at the T-junction onto White Street, which soon bends left. Turn right by metal railings into the churchyard of St Mary the Virgin and turn left where the path meets the road. Now retrace your steps, turning left past the King's Head, to the car park.

Place of Interest
Thrigby Hall Wildlife Gardens are 6½ miles from Martham, off the A1064, near Filby. This zoo, set in the attractive grounds of an 18th century hall, specializes in breeding endangered species, including Sumatran tigers. Telephone: 01493 369477.

Date walk completed:
....

The White Horse

One of the great attractions walking in Norfolk has to offer is the range of riverside paths taking you over open, unspoilt country-side with huge sky-scapes and a rich variety of wildlife. This route is a good example as it follows first the busy Yare and then the Chet, its tributary, before arriving at the picturesque setting of Hardley Flood. One of Norfolk's special round-towered churches, simply beautiful, completes the picture.

The White Horse has been at the heart of village life for well over 100 years. It is a comfortable, welcoming pub, with a couple of bars, an attractive dining area, a patio and garden. Food is mainly traditional – homemade steak and kidney pie, and Barnsley chop, for example – with more exotic dishes such as a seafood elite. At least four real ales are normally available, regulars being Adnams Best and Broadside, Ridleys IPA and Flowers Original.

Opening times are from 11 am to 4 pm and from 6 pm to 11 pm and food is served from noon to 1.45 pm and from 6 pm to 9 pm. No food is served on Monday lunchtimes in winter (check with the pub for exact dates).

Telephone: 01508 520250.

Distance: *4½ miles*

OS Landranger 134 Norwich and the Broads or OS Explorer OL40 The Broads GR 388013

An easy walk, but muddy in places

Starting point: The car park at Hardley Staithe, near Chedgrave.

How to get there: Chedgrave is 10 miles south-east of Norwich, signed left off the A146. As you come into the village, you pass the White Horse pub on your right; then turn immediately left (signed to Hardley Street) and first right (signed to Hardley). Keep on this road, ignoring all turns, until you reach Hardley Staithe. Parking is on a grassy area to the right.

The Walk

1 Go straight ahead, keeping Hardley Dyke on your left. This channel was cut between 1810 and 1840 to provide a good link with the nearby River Yare for loading and unloading goods, though it seems there had been a staithe of sorts here since Saxon times. Away to your left, you can see the chimney of Cantley sugar refinery (in full operation between late October and February) as you go over a stile with a Broads Authority yellow arrow. The good grassy path bends now to run alongside the Yare. (To your right, an expanse of grazing marsh criss-crossed by narrow dykes spreads out below, and,

across the river, an old windpump tower is a good place for cormorants to perch.) A huge loop in the path then brings you to the junction of the Yare and the Chet. (Here Hardley Cross makes an ideal resting and boat-watching point. The stone cross, which bears a date of 1676 (restored in 1820), marks the ancient boundary between the jurisdiction on the Yare of the City of Norwich and the Borough of Great Yarmouth.

2 The path now turns right to run alongside the Chet, looping right and left to follow the river. (This is good bird-watching territory at any time of the year, my latest visit, in November, being

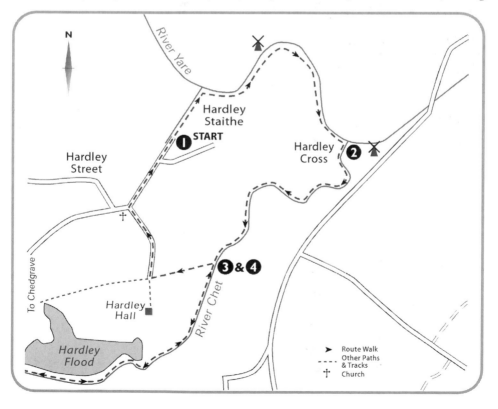

rewarded with a family of Bewick's swans, a curlew, a grey heron, a bush full of fieldfare and a low-flying green woodpecker all within a short stretch of path.) There now follows a series of stiles over a fairly short distance. After the fourth stile, there is a track heading off to the right by an area of concrete hard-standing. Ignore this for the moment and keep straight ahead beside the river.

3 The path runs straight now for about a quarter of a mile before entering the unusual setting of Hardley Flood. With the river still on your left, a large expanse of water appears on your right, the gap between the two only a matter of a few yards, so that occasionally, at very high tides, the way becomes impassable. Walk the half a mile or so along the length of the water; this is a beautiful place, often crammed with wildfowl. At the end of the lake (or before if you wish to shorten the walk), turn and retrace your steps to the track mentioned earlier.

4 Turn left on the broad track, marked by a yellow Norfolk County Council arrow, and, after a gentle climb, pass Hill Cottage on your right. After a further 200 yards (here you can see Hardley Hall below to your left), turn right on a metalled lane (Hardley Hall Lane). Before turning right at the T-junction onto Hardley Staithe Road, a detour of a few yards to your left to look at St Margaret's church is strongly recommended. (This church with its Norman round tower is an unspoilt delight. There is a fine 15th century wall painting showing St Christopher carrying Jesus on his shoulder while fish swim round his feet, and a smaller depiction of St Catherine bearing her wheel emblem.

Hardley Cross, an ancient river boundary marker

The ancient pine pews have aged well and in earlier times provided a canvas for children – presumably bored by the sermons – to scratch the outlines of the boats that traded on the nearby river.) Follow Hardley Staithe Road, passing farm buildings on your right, to return to your starting point.

Place of Interest

Hales Hall Barn and Gardens, 3 miles south of Chedgrave and signed off the A146, is the largest medieval brick barn in England. Built in 1480, it belonged to a hall. In the grounds are a moat, lawns and borders, topiary and conservatories, and a nursery specializing in rare and exotic conservatory plants and fruit.

Date walk completed:

. . . .